Thoughtful Christianity

Thoughtful Christianity

Faith and Action in the Way of Jesus

BEN DANIEL

WESTMINSTER
JOHN KNOX PRESS
LOUISVILLE · KENTUCKY

© 2015 Ben Daniel

First edition
Published by Westminster John Knox Press
Louisville, Kentucky

15 16 17 18 19 20 21 22 23 24—10 9 8 7 6 5 4 3 2 1

Scripture quotations from the New Revised Standard Version of the Bible are copyright © 1989 by the Division of Christian Education of the National Council of the Churches of Christ in the U.S.A. and are used by permission.

Book design by Drew Stevens
Cover design by designpointinc.com
Cover photo ©iStock.com/Rozaliya

Library of Congress Cataloging-in-Publication Data

Daniel, Ben.
  Thoughtful Christianity : faith and action in the way of Jesus / Ben Daniel. -- First edition.
    pages cm
  ISBN 978-0-664-26064-4 (alk. paper)
  1. Thought and thinking--Religious aspects--Christianity. 2. Christianity--Philosophy.
I. Title.
  BV4598.4.D36 2015
  230--dc23
                                                                                2015012607

♾ The paper used in this publication meets the minimum requirements
of the American National Standard for Information Sciences—Permanence of Paper
for Printed Library Materials, ANSI Z39.48-1992.

Most Westminster John Knox Press books are available at special quantity discounts
when purchased in bulk by corporations, organizations, and special-interest groups.
For more information, please e-mail SpecialSales@wjkbooks.com.

For Karen and Michael Moreland,
with gratitude and love

Journeys are the midwives of thought.
—Alain de Botton, *The Art of Travel*

Contents

Acknowledgments

The title of this book, *Thoughtful Christianity*, connects what's written in these pages to a website with a similar name that, like Westminster John Knox Press, belongs to the Presbyterian Publishing Corporation. TheThoughtfulChristian.com is an online retail space and a great resource for those of any denomination who are looking for books, Christian education curricula for all ages, study guides, and liturgical resources. When the good folks at Westminster John Knox invited me to write a book that would explore what it means to be a "Thoughtful Christian," it was a profound honor—and it scared me a little bit. At my ordination as a Minister of Word and Sacrament (what we now call a Teaching Elder) I took a vow to "further the peace, unity, and purity of the Church." The Presbyterian Publishing Corporation, by trusting me with their brand, has given me ample opportunity to break that particular vow. However, they also gave me the opportunity to write this book under the gentle guidance of my editor, Jessica Miller Kelley. Sometimes a coconspirator, sometimes a referee, always wise, Jessica has been great. I am grateful for the trust of the Presbyterian Publishing Corporation and for Jessica's editorial excellence.

I am aware of no well-written book that sprang forth from the ether of its author's mind without the help of others. This book is no exception. I'm grateful to Professor Jim Bennett of Santa Clara University who, besides being a kind and supportive friend, also introduced me to his colleague, David Pleins, a Darwin scholar who was exceptionally generous with his time and his insights as I tried to wrap my head around Darwin's religious views. The Rev. Winnie Gordon of Shrewsbury's

Unitarian church also was generous with her time and with her knowledge of the history of Unitarianism. I'm grateful to Professor John Eby of Loras College in Dubuque, Iowa, who has helped me understand the medieval mind and the history of the Crusades; to Dr. Cynthia Cudeback, an oceanographer who helped me think through the importance of empiricism (and who acted as a spiritual director in the process); and to Tyler Grinberg, who helped reassure me when I started to doubt the validity of some of my scientific claims. (Tyler, who teaches high school science, is married to my niece; it's always good for a pastor to have a scientist in the family.)

As I wrote this book I borrowed stories from friends and relatives. Sometimes this has been outright appropriation and sometimes I have written about times when my story has intersected with theirs. I am grateful to Job and his family; to my brother Morgan Daniel; to Patrick Rickon; to my mother-in-law, Patricia Sheffey; to Christine Letcher and Julia McDonald; and to members of the Faith Trio in Oakland, California, a group I am late to join but whose Presbyterian, Reform Jewish, and Shiite Muslim members have been coming together for conversation and fellowship since the dark days following September 11, 2001.

Once, in the face of intractable writer's block, I also borrowed a few paragraphs from something I'd written for another publisher. In 2013 I wrote the study guide for *The Jesus Fatwa*, a series of videos that addresses Islamophobia in the United States. David Felten and Jeff Procter-Murphy of Living the Questions were kind enough to allow me to put some of what I had written for them into this book (for more information on *The Jesus Fatwa* and Living the Questions' other fine video curricula, please visit www.livingthequestions.com).

For much of this book I drew inspiration from various travels I've made over the years. I am particularly grateful to my brother Patrick Moreland, who joined me on a trip to Switzerland and France in the winter of 2013. In Scotland, my friends Craig Smith and Michelle Thomson-Smith welcomed me into their home and offered me incomparable hospitality and a friendship filled with laughter and a shared desire to heal a broken world. Thank you, dear friends, and *saor Alba*! In Scotland I also enjoyed the hospitality of the Iona Community, who welcomed me to their Abbey and gave me a place of quiet where I could write the final words of this book's first draft.

I wrote this book in lots of different places, but some of the best writing happened on the shores of Monterey Bay at a beach house my friends Glenda Parmentier and Jane Wallace lent to my family during the summer of 2014. Sand that lingers in the pages of my copy of Niebuhr's *Christ and Culture* reminds me of the magical time we spent at Pajaro Dunes.

During the development and writing of this book I served as pastor to two congregations. In the early stages of planning the book I was the pastor of Foothill Presbyterian Church in San José, California, a post I held for more than sixteen years; just before I started writing the book I changed jobs and started working as the pastor of Montclair Presbyterian Church in Oakland. I am grateful to the sessions, congregations, and staffs of both churches for their kind and enthusiastic support. They have given me space to write and have allowed me to make creative and unorthodox use of study-leave funds to finance my travels.

My deepest thanks goes to those I love most. I am grateful to my children, Mimi, Nellie and William, who, on top of being pastor's kids, also have a dad who on occasion disappears to write; and more than anything I owe a debt of love and gratitude to my wife, Anne Marie, who is my first editor, my kindest and most trustworthy critic, my staunchest supporter, and my truest friend. Everything in my life that is marked by beauty, tenderness, and joy comes as a result of the good fortune that is mine because I share my life with her.

Ben Daniel
The Abbey,
Iona, Argyle,
Scotland

Introduction

The United States is, by many measures, the most religious country in the industrialized Western world. Nearly 60 percent of us claim religion to be an important part of our lives (by contrast, only 13 percent of the population in France and 19 percent of the UK considers itself religious), but when it comes to religious knowledge, Americans are, on average, about as dense as a loaf of pumpernickel.

In 2010, the Pew Forum on Religion and Public Life released a study that gauged American religious literacy by giving 3,412 randomly selected Americans a test of 32 questions with which to assess what participants in the survey knew about religion. On average, the Americans surveyed answered about half of the questions correctly. Ironically, the cohort of Americans who knew the most about religion were the atheists (who got about 21 out of 32 answers correct, which still isn't great), followed by Jews (20.5 out of 32) and Mormons (20.1 out of 32). White mainline Protestants, on average, answered fewer than half of the questions correctly, behind evangelical Protestants and white Catholics and ahead of black Protestants, those who claimed no religious identity, and Hispanic Catholics.

Among the most interesting findings in the Pew Center's study is that while Americans, understandably perhaps, are ignorant about the content of the faiths they do not practice (only half of the responders knew the Dalai Lama is Buddhist, for example), the study also showed that Americans are just as ignorant about their own traditions. Fewer than half of the surveyed Protestants identified Martin Luther as the founder of the Protestant movement, and fewer than 20 percent knew that "salvation by faith alone" is a key tenet of Protestant theology.[1]

A similar paucity of Jews could identify Maimonides—the great twelfth-century Talmudic scholar—as being Jewish, and most Catholics didn't know their Church believes in transubstantiation—the conversion, during the mass, of bread and wine into the actual body and blood of Christ.

Religion is not unique among subjects about which Americans lack knowledge. Our understanding of geography is similarly atrocious: a poll conducted in 2006, for example, found that fewer than half of Americans aged 18 to 24 could identify the location of Iraq, and only one in ten Americans could find Afghanistan on a map of Asia;[2] a person might be justified in suspecting similar results for polls assessing American's knowledge of history or biology.

What sets our lack of religious knowledge apart is that when it comes to matters of religion, ignorance proves no inhibition for American Christians hell-bent on using political strength to bend public policy so that it complies with the tenets of Christianity—not as it has been practiced in the past but as they have misunderstood it in the present. Christians with little real knowledge of what the Bible says in its various and conflicting creation stories and who don't understand basic science still work tirelessly to restrict the teaching of evolutionary biology in public schools. Protestants unfamiliar with the Reformation's suspicion of earthly power embrace an unquestioning patriotism and support wars (being carried out in places they cannot find on a map) that would be unacceptable under any traditional reading of Christian just war theory. Meanwhile, those Christians who might otherwise speak out against such abuses of ignorant faith are unfamiliar with the prophetic traditions that gave rise to the civil rights movement (to say nothing of the abolition of the transatlantic slave trade, the Reformation, or the birth of Christianity itself); they insist religion and politics must not mix and they say very little that is helpful in our nation's ongoing civic conversation.

It is clear to me that American Christians are long overdue for a great awakening of the mind. Whereas previous nationwide revivals have filled empty pews with repentant rear ends

by way of tents pitched on the prairie by itinerant evangelists
or by using football stadiums filled to capacity by those eager
for the eternal comforts served up by Brylcreemed crusaders,
the next revival must be an awakening in the intellect of Christians ready to mark the life of the Church and of the broader
society with a thoughtful faith.

This great awakening of thoughtfulness must necessarily
include a commitment to education and to learning as a way of
life. In order to refresh our minds with thoughtfulness, Christians must place curiosity in high esteem and must value faith
communities where substantive conversations are a meaningful
part of spiritual formation. We must celebrate doubters and
honor those with the humility to admit they may be wrong. We
must be instructed by those with the courage to be corrected.

The education necessary for a reawakening of thoughtful Christianity must include a willingness on the part of the
thoughtful Christian to allow his or her faith to be informed
and formed by secular, empirical knowledge, and it must
include a dedicated commitment to relearning and to reen-
gaging with the theological insights and spiritual wisdom of
Christian tradition.

To long for such an awakening of thoughtful faith is not to
wish for the *birth* of thoughtful faith; after all, there is nothing new or particularly revolutionary around the idea that the
work of loving God with one's mind is basic to the life of faith.[3]
Thoughtful Christianity has become drowsy of late, however,
and as a result, the religious landscape increasingly is dominated by forms of Christianity that shun intellectual endeavors,
are skeptical of science and of other forms of empirical learning, or lack a distinctively Christian voice because they ignore
the history and the traditions that for centuries have shaped the
Christian faith.

The ambition of this book is not so much to lead or to
define the much-needed revival of thoughtful Christianity
in America, for indeed the movement already is afoot and is
blessed with many eloquent spokespersons. Rather, this vol-
ume is an attempt to pledge allegiance to the company of those

who would love God with their minds and to provide an artic-
ulation of thoughtful Christianity that may prove useful for
others who wish to join in the journey toward a beloved community animated and fortified by thoughtful faith.

TOWARD AN AWAKENING

To write a book calling for the reawakening of thoughtful faith
is to face certain temptations, and chief among them is a temp-
tation to scold evangelical Christians for their seeming inability
to be informed by scientific common sense and to reprimand
progressive Christians for their apparent indifference to the
wisdom of tradition.

Such temptations are understandable. After all, the modern evangelicalism that so dominates contemporary American
Protestantism finds its origins in a Victorian-era rejection of
modern scientific progress[4] whose legacy can be found in an
ongoing skepticism of evolutionary biology, a willingness to
doubt the reality of climate change, a reticence to vaccinate
girls against the cancer-causing human papillomavirus, and a
refusal to see homosexuality as anything but a psychological
deviance for which there must be a cure.[5]

Meanwhile, modern progressive Protestantism, starting with
a willingness to accommodate Darwin's theories on the origins
of species, has drawn strength from a comfortable conversation with science and with other forms of empirical intellectual
inquiry, but somewhere along the way many progressives wan-
dered far from the watershed of history and tradition that feeds
the streams of faith. As a result, progressive churches, in their
longing for social justice and societal transformation, take their
ideological cues from the politics of the secular left and
their rhetorical promptings from the inoffensive-yet-poetically-
flat language of academia. Many progressive Christians have
a lot to offer the world as secular liberals, but as people of
faith they know little and say less about what the wisdom of
the Church forged though centuries of struggle and success,

suffering and joy, may bring to the project of making the world a better place for all of God's children.

In the end, when it comes to evangelicals and progressives, a certain amount of criticism can go both ways. The evangelical who agitates for draconian and punitive immigration laws has not been informed by the traditions of her faith—particularly those found in the Bible's injunctions to welcome strangers, to include sojourners in the life of the community, and to remember our own status as "strangers in a strange land" in our dealings with others; the progressive who insists on clinging to the notion that Islam is inherently and exceptionally misogynistic may consciously be ignoring empirical data readily available to those willing to talk directly with Muslim women.

Tempting also is the siren song of the middle way. In a world broken asunder by the clash of extremes, moderation and balance have their charms, yet this book is not an argument for a moderate faith, for to seek comfort in the middle is to be subjected to the whims of the extremes, whose ever-changing radicalism makes centrist balance an impossible dream.

The Christian in search of a righteous middle ground also must face the uncomfortable reality that moderation lends validity to the fringes between which the moderate wants to find balance. The moderate who craves the input of a wide variety of perspectives may hesitate before taking a faithful stand that might alienate those at the far end of an ideological spectrum. Such a craving for balance lacks the fortitude necessary to move the Church into the realm of the Beloved Community. This longing for a bland middle ground is, in part, why Martin Luther King Jr. famously wrote that he'd nearly reached the conclusion that the greatest threat to the cause of civil rights was not the white racist but the white moderate,

> who is more devoted to "order" than to justice; who prefers a negative peace which is the absence of tension to a positive peace which is the presence of justice; who constantly says: "I agree with you in the goal you seek, but I cannot agree with your methods of direct action"; who paternalistically believes he can set the timetable for another man's freedom;

who lives by a mythical concept of time and who constantly advises the Negro to wait for a "more convenient season."[6]

Though this book was written by a pastor who long ago set aside the evangelicalism of his youth and now preaches from one of America's most liberal Presbyterian pulpits, it is not meant to be a simple endorsement of the Christian left, nor is it a blanket condemnation of the Christian right. Neither is it a centrist manifesto. Rather, this book hopes to point American Christians to faith as it existed before the establishment of our current categories. It hopes to revive an approach to religion that has fainted for a lack of intellectual food.

To revive a thoughtful faith is to awaken the spirit of many of the greatest heroes of Christian history—the apostle Paul, the Church Fathers, St. Augustine, Hildegard von Bingen, Martin Luther, John Calvin, Marguerite de Navarre, Sor Juana Inez de la Cruz, the brothers Wesley, William Wilberforce, Harriet Beecher Stowe and her brother Henry Ward Beecher, Albert Schweitzer, and Martin Luther King Jr. (to name just a few)— all were people whose faith was rooted in a sound knowledge of tradition and formed by intelligence, curiosity, and secular learning.

Given the anti-intellectual mood of contemporary American culture and the general lack of religious knowledge, and given the tremendous complexity of the problems that face the world in which we live, the time has come for American Christians to embrace thoughtfulness as a way of forming faith. Because it is informed by objective information and empirical knowledge, and because it is formed by the spiritual traditions that give Christianity a unique voice, a thoughtful faith is better able to meet the challenges of life in a world forever at war, a nation of increasing economic disparity, and a Church so riven by conflict that it is unable to speak a meaningful word of peace in a violent world, a Church so appropriated by economies of greed that it has no prophetic voice with which to call down the waters of justice in a world of hunger, want, and need.

Ours, in short, is a time that longs for the refreshment that thoughtful faith can provide once it awakens. The good news— the promise even—is that thoughtful faith, with all of its truth, beauty, and goodness, can awaken in each of us. This book hopes to be one of many crowing roosters that will, finally, get the mind of the Church—and each of us within it—out of bed and ready to face the day that is dawning.

PART I

The Evolution of a Divided Christian Community

1

The Accidental Schism

I had no intention to write atheistically.
—Charles Darwin, in a letter to American
botanist Asa Gray[1]

Tucked snugly in an omega-shaped curve in the River Severn, Shrewsbury is a small city with all of the charm an American wants to find in England: there's a castle; several tall-spired, Gothic churches (remodeled in the nineteenth century with Victorian sentimentality); plenty of half-timbered buildings standing side by side, listing slightly. In those buildings are excellent bookstores, great restaurants, chichi boutiques, and pubs in which a person can get beer pumped straight from the cask and steak and ale pie, the eating of which (and I speak from experience here) is a transcendent experience. Just down the street from one such pub—The Wheat Sheave—and across the street from a darling stationery store with an nice selection of fountain pens is Shrewsbury's Unitarian church, the building that brought me to this lovely town.

Any book dealing with the question of what it means for Christians to practice a thoughtful faith must address the relationship between religion and science and, at least in the American context, any discussion about the interplay between secular discovery and theological insight is a journey that must, at some point, go through the Unitarian church in Shrewsbury, for as much as it may seem hard to believe of a small church in a town with a vibe that feels more Dickens than, say, Dawkins, the Unitarian church in Shrewsbury played a small but vital role in launching a movement that would shake Christianity to its core, driving a wedge into the heart of the Church, dividing the faithful between those who are comfortable incorporating modernism into religious practice and those who feel secular, scientific insights pose a threat to Christian truth claims by undermining the authority of Scripture. The Unitarian church in Shrewsbury played a part in setting up this great controversy by being the place where Charles Darwin, the great and controversial evolutionary biologist, received his earliest religious instruction.

A pilgrim in search of a shrine that commemorates and honors the father of modern evolutionary biology has many options. He could visit Darwin's childhood home just outside Shrewsbury or she could travel to Down House, in Kent, where Charles and Anna Darwin raised an impressive brood of children and where the great biologist wrote his most important books. More adventurous pilgrims could visit the Galápagos Islands off the west coast of South America, where Darwin made significant observations that, much later, would lead him to develop his groundbreaking theories. I chose instead to visit Darwin's childhood church because the building stands as a reminder that thoughtful Christians need not be threatened by Darwin's scientific insights. Though he knew many religious folks would be troubled by what he proposed, Darwin was not hostile to Christianity, and his work was not intended to cause offense. The Christian rift that followed the publication of Darwin's work was not at all what Darwin had in mind and—for thoughtful Christians—it was (and still is) entirely unnecessary.

Today, the congregation of the Unitarian church in Shrewsbury is too small to employ a full-time minister. Their Sunday morning services are either lay-run or led by visiting clergy. Once a month, the Rev. Winnie Gordon comes up from Birmingham during the week to meet with parishioners and to provide pastoral care. Winnie's parents immigrated to England from Jamaica. She has a big smile and an easy laugh. She practices a progressive faith, but her spiritual embrace is wide enough that she follows the podcasts of a prominent Californian megachurch that severed its ties to the Presbyterian Church (U.S.A.) when the denomination opened its pulpits to preachers who self-identify as gay men or lesbians.

I was in Shrewsbury on the one day in the month of November when the Unitarian church was open midweek. When I walked in Rev. Gordon was just finishing up a meeting with a small group of parishioners, but she was quick to greet me and to offer me a tour of the sanctuary—not a long tour, mind you, because the space is small, but sufficient to get a sense for the history of the place.

The congregation got its start in 1662, when—during the Restoration of Charles II—the Church of England excommunicated two of Shrewsbury's more prominent clergymen, who refused to use the *Book of Common Prayer* in worship or to affirm the thirty-nine articles of the Anglican faith. The two defrocked pastors, together with members of their former congregations, came together to establish a Presbyterian church in which they were free to walk in closer communion with Calvin.

In Shrewsbury, Presbyterianism survived mobs of marauding Jacobites, who destroyed their sanctuary in 1715, but it could not endure the open-mindedness of the local population. By late in the 1700s Reformed theology gave way to freethinking Unitarianism, which survives to this day under the part-time ministry of Winnie Gordon, who, when she preaches in Shrewsbury, does so from the same pulpit Samuel Taylor Coleridge used when he was applying for the job of pastor to the Shrewsbury congregation, a position he decided not to take when one of the congregation's prominent members, Josiah Wedgwood (a potter and purveyor of fine china to European nobility), offered to pay the young seminarian a stipend so he could concentrate on writing poetry instead of pursuing the life of a pastor.

Besides being a potter and a patron of poetry, Josiah Wedgwood also had the distinction of being the grandfather of Charles Darwin, Shrewsbury's most prominent son and, by far, the most famous person ever to attend the Shrewsbury Unitarian Church. Darwin attended the Shrewsbury Unitarian Church from his birth in 1809 until his eighth year, when young Charles's mother, Susanna Darwin (nee Wedgwood), died and the future biologist's father started taking the family to St. Mary's, the Church of England congregation just up the hill from the Unitarians.

Darwin's father was a physician and person of means (helped, in no small measure, by marrying into the Wedgwood clan), and he expected his second son, Charles, after a comfortable upbringing, to follow him in the practice of medicine. But the younger Darwin, whose interest in the natural world began in childhood, had little desire to study medicine. He wanted, instead, to collect and examine bugs, which led him—curiously—after a failed attempt to feign interest in medicine at the University of Edinburgh, to the study of theology at Cambridge.

Actually, Darwin's decision to study theology probably had two motivations. First, Darwin seems to have assumed that life in a parsonage would be not so much pastoral (as in, interacting with the needs and occasional demands of parishioners) as pastoral (as in, a tranquil life of contemplation lived in beautiful open spaces), with plenty of time during which to chase down beetles. Second, while studying at Cambridge, Darwin seems to have been drawn to the field of natural theology, a field of study rooted in the confidence that a person can learn about God by studying God's handiwork in creation.

Natural theology was a perfect fit for someone like Darwin, who had some interest in metaphysical questions but who, truth be told, was really more interested in insects. Thanks to the insights of natural theologians such as William Paley, a person could collect and classify bugs and call it a theological education. This was perfect for Charles Darwin, and while Darwin's theological insights were keen and his interest in religion survived his personal faith, he was more of a scientist than a theologian. Darwin's observations of the natural world and his abilities as a collector, curator, and studier of biological specimens gained him a strong enough reputation as a scientist that he was able, at the age of twenty-two, to join an expedition on the *HMS Beagle* as it set out to make better maps of the South American coastline.

Darwin was something of a "staff scientist" onboard the *Beagle*, and he used the journey—which eventually circumnavigated the globe—as an opportunity to make observations about plants, animals, and human customs in parts of the world which, at the time, were relatively unknown to Europeans. Some of Darwin's observations on the *Beagle's* voyage—in combination with later data collected from decades devoted to studying the specimens collected on the journey—led Darwin to conclude that species living today have evolved, adapting by a process of natural selection rather than having been designed and created by God in their current forms, without the possibility of mutation.

Darwin's conclusions relative to evolution were years in the making. His observations were precise, his analysis was meticulous, and his attention to detail was extraordinary. Besides, he was a man with many interests (in addition to beetles and bird beaks, he was passionate about barnacles and beekeeping); he had eight children and an estate that needed his attention, but eventually—after twenty-three years of thinking about it—Darwin wrote and published his theories about evolution in two books, *On the Origin of Species by Means of Natural Selection, or the Preservation of Favoured Races in the Struggle for Life* (1859) and, twelve years later, *The Descent of Man, and Selection in Relation to Sex*. In *The Origin of Species* Darwin articulated general ideas about how species evolve; in *The Descent of Man*, he applied his theories of evolution to human development. Both books were wildly popular and profoundly controversial.

WHAT'S THE BIG DEAL?

It's worth asking why Darwin's work caused such a fuss. After all, for everything Darwin discovered, and for all his work as a scientist, his ideas, though revolutionary, did not occur in a scientific vacuum. Darwin's contributions to the field of biology were not the work of a lone, misunderstood maverick, a mad scientist seeing things no one else had observed and asking questions that had occurred to no one else. Rather, Darwin was part of a well-established scientific community that, though centered in London, was global in its reach. His work was vetted by his peers, who included some of the very best minds of his day.

Darwin was hardly the first person publicly to posit ideas that challenged the existence of God. Nineteen years before Darwin left Shrewsbury to travel around the world in the *Beagle*, faculty members of the Presbyterian-affiliated College of New Jersey in Princeton (now Princeton University) had grown so comfortable with (then-modern) enlightenment philosophy that traditionalist forces within the Presbyterian Church both sacked the college's president and established a theological seminary (Princeton Theological Seminary) a few blocks from the university to ensure prospective clergymen would study theology in a pristine environment unmarred by secular speculation.[2] By the time Darwin's books made it onto the shelves of the world's libraries and booksellers, secular and religious scholarship already were comfortably at odds. Darwin did not create the rift between religion and science.

Nor did Darwin invent the idea of evolution; rather, he described it better than anyone who had come before, and he offered the most compelling and convincing arguments for it. While it's true that one cannot embrace Darwin's theories of evolution while believing that the first chapter of Genesis offers up an account of creation that is both historically accurate and scientifically reliable, by the time Darwin came along, many faithful readers of Genesis had long since given up looking to Genesis for empirical data about the origins of life on earth.

Some three hundred years before Darwin wrote *The Origin of Species* and *The Descent of Man*, no less a lover of the Bible than John Calvin was unbothered by the ways science renders Genesis useless as a textbook for scientific history. In his commentary on Genesis 1:16 ("God made the two great lights—the greater light to rule the day and the lesser light to rule the night—and the stars"), Calvin wrote,

> Moses makes two great luminaries; but astronomers prove, by conclusive reasons, that the star of Saturn, which on account of its great distance, appears the least of all, is greater than the moon. Here lies the difference; Moses wrote in a popular style things which without instruction, all ordinary persons, endued with common sense, are able to understand; but astronomers investigate with great labor whatever the sagacity of the human mind can comprehend. Nevertheless, this study is not to be reprobated, nor this science to be condemned, because some frantic persons are wont boldly to reject whatever is unknown to them. For astronomy is not only pleasant, but also very useful to be known: it cannot be denied that this art unfolds the admirable wisdom of God. Wherefore, as ingenious men are to be honored who have expended useful labor on this subject, so they who have leisure and capacity ought not to neglect this kind of exercise.[3]

And if Calvin's embrace of science and a nonliteral reading of Genesis—published a year before Galileo's birth—seems a surprise, consider this: thirteen hundred years before Calvin (and sixteen hundred years before Darwin), Origen of Alexandria, one of the Church Fathers, wrote,

> Now who is there, pray, possessed of understanding, that will regard the statement as appropriate, that the first day, and the second, and the third, in which also both evening and morning are mentioned, existed without sun, and moon, and stars—the first day even without a sky? And who is found so ignorant as to suppose that God, as if He had been a husbandman, planted trees in paradise, in Eden towards the east, and a tree of life in it, i.e., a visible and palpable tree of wood, so that anyone eating of it with bodily teeth should obtain life, and, eating again of another tree, should come to the knowledge of good and evil? No one, I think, can doubt that the statement that God walked in the

afternoon in paradise, and that Adam lay hid under a tree, is related figuratively in Scripture, that some mystical meaning may be indicated by it. The departure of Cain from the presence of the Lord will manifestly cause a careful reader to inquire what is the presence of God, and how anyone can go out from it. But not to extend the task which we have before us beyond its due limits, it is very easy for anyone who pleases to gather out of holy Scripture what is recorded indeed as having been done, but what nevertheless cannot be believed as having reasonably and appropriately occurred according to the historical account.[4]

Darwin's scientific discoveries led him away from a belief in God, at least as God is understood in the Christian tradition, but this disbelief probably was rooted in personal experience as much as in science. In 1851 he lost a daughter to tuberculosis, an experience that can unsettle the faith of even the most devout. Yet while scientific observation and personal experience led Darwin away from his childhood devotion, he was not hostile toward religion, as many of his now-opponents would like to imagine. As noted above, his university degree was in theology, not in biology, and throughout his life—long after his journeys on the *Beagle*—he provided generous financial support for the work of Anglican missionaries in South America.[5] Many of Darwin's close associates (most notably his wife) continued to practice a life of faith, and Darwin was supportive. In fact, Darwin's staunchest ally in the United States was the botanist Asa Gray, a professor at Harvard and one of America's leading scientists at the time. Gray was a devout Christian who saw no conflict between his faith and Darwin's theories of evolution. Gray's writings on the compatibility of faith and evolution so impressed Darwin that Darwin collected them and had them published in England.[6]

THE REVERBERATIONS OF DARWIN'S WORK

Yet Darwin's work caused a religious scandal so powerful, one can feel its reverberations today, even outside of the Church.

In the popular American imagination, the watershed moment for Darwin's theory of evolution came in 1925 in Dayton, Tennessee, when a high school teacher by the name of John Scopes was arrested and put on trial for teaching evolution in violation of Tennessee law. Though Dayton, Tennessee, is a small town that today has just over 7,300 residents with a median household income that in 2012 was just under the poverty level for a family of five,[7] the trial was a big deal. The great journalist and social critic H. L. Mencken covered the proceedings for the *New York Times*. The opposing sides imported two of the nation's greatest lawyers: William Jennings Bryan, a former Secretary of State and three-time presidential candidate, for the prosecution and Clarence Darrow, "a notorious agnostic, and a leading defender of underdogs and progressive learning"[8] representing the twenty-four-year-old Scopes in what would prove to be a legal failure but a cultural victory for the modernist cause.

The trial was a showdown between fundamentalism and modernism that served as a proxy conflict for the ongoing antagonism between northern and southern states and between urban and rural America. It was, according to historian George M. Marsden, an event with all "the elements of a great American drama—farce, comedy, tragedy, and pathos."[9] Marsden writes,

> The central theme was, inescapably, the clash of two worlds, the rural and the urban. In the popular imagination there were on the one side the small town, the backwoods, half-educated yokels, obscurantism, crackpot hawkers of religion, fundamentalism, the South and the personification of the agrarian myth himself, William Jennings Bryan. Opposed to these were the city, the clique of New York-Chicago lawyers, intellectuals, journalists, wits, sophisticates, modernists and the cynical agnostic Clarence Darrow. These images evoked the familiar experiences of millions of Americans who had been born in the country and moved to the city or who were at least witnessing the dramatic shift from a predominantly rural to a predominantly urban culture.[10]

The trial came to be known as the Scopes Monkey Trial, and most Americans' knowledge of the trial itself comes from the 1955 play and subsequent movie *Inherit the Wind*, neither of which (properly, in my opinion) let strict historical accuracy get in the way of a solid dramatic narrative.

Oddly, John Scopes, the defendant in the monkey trial that bears his name, got in trouble for teaching evolution using a textbook, *A Civic Biology Presented in Problems,* by George William Hunter that the Tennessee Board of Education mandated for use in the state's high schools, in contradiction to the state's own laws.[11] The book, which was published in 1914, is interesting and at times alarming. After making its presentation of evolutionary biology, in a chapter called "Heredity and Variation" there is a passage that reads,

> When people marry there are certain things that the individual as well as the whole race should demand. The most important of these is freedom from germ diseases which might be handed down to offspring. Tuberculosis, that dread white plague which is still responsible for one seventh of all deaths, epilepsy, and feeblemindedness are handicaps which it is not only unfair but criminal to hand down to posterity. The science of being well-born is called *eugenics.*
>
> Studies have been made on a number of different families in this country, in which mental and moral defects were present in one or both of the original parents. The "Jukes" family is a notorious example. The first mother is known as "Margaret, mother of criminals." In seventy-five years the progeny of the original generation has cost the state of New York over a million and a quarter of dollars, besides giving over to the care of prisons and asylums considerably over a hundred feeble-minded, alcoholic, immoral, or criminal persons. Another case recently studied is the "Kallikak" family. This family has been traced to the union of Martin Kallikak, a young soldier of the War of the Revolution, with a feeble-minded girl. She had a feeble-minded son from whom there have been to the present time 480 descendants. Of these 33 were sexually immoral, 24 confirmed drunkards, 3 epileptics, and 143 *feeble-minded.* The man who started this terrible line of immorality and feeble-mindedness later married a normal Quaker girl. From

this couple a line of 496 descendants have come, with *no* cases of feeble-mindedness. The evidence and the moral speak for themselves!

Hundreds of families such as those described above exist to-day, spreading disease, immorality, and crime to all parts of this country. The cost to society of such families is very severe. Just as certain animals or plants become parasitic on other plants or animals, these families have become parasitic on society. They not only do harm to others by corrupting, stealing or spreading disease, but they are actually protected and cared for by the state out of public money. Largely for them the poorhouse and asylum exist. They take from the society but give nothing in return. They are parasites.

If such people were lower animals, we would probably kill them off to prevent them from spreading. Humanity will not allow this, but we do have the remedy of separating the sexes in asylums or in other places and in various ways preventing intermarriage and the possibilities of perpetuating such a low and degenerate race. Remedies of this sort have been tried successfully in Europe and are now meeting with success in this country.[12]

What's remarkable about this passage is not that it validates Darwin's work on evolution (it doesn't—*A Civic Biology* teaches about evolution in an earlier chapter), but that folks on both sides of the evolution debate either missed this endorsement of eugenics or deemed it unworthy of comment. Even today, in a post-Holocaust world, the textbook's support for scientific ideas that helped lay the foundation for Hitler's "final solution" usually eludes the notice of those whose minds otherwise are occupied worrying about primates in the family tree. When addressing the use of *A Civic Biology Presented in Problems* as a textbook for high school students in Tennessee, religious folk, it turns out were—and in many cases still are—asking the wrong questions, and secular folk aren't asking questions at all. That fundamentalists deem Scopes's teaching of eugenics unworthy of protest and that secular liberals continue to celebrate Scopes and Darrow despite the evil underbelly of what was happening in the Dayton, Tennessee, classroom should make any thoughtful Christian think twice before celebrating the Scopes Monkey Trial as an unambiguous victory for science and the cause of progress.

MYOPIC HINDSIGHT

The overlooked endorsement of eugenics in *A Civic Biology* raises important questions about why Darwin and his theories have been so extraordinarily problematic for Christians. A thoughtful faith might overlook Darwin's ultimately non-threatening scientific ideas and focus instead on what truly is heinous in the textbook, but since the middle of the nineteenth century, Christians—even Christians who otherwise have demonstrated great thoughtfulness—have been arguing over theories never intended to cause religious disruption.

Looking for an answer to why Darwin's theories have proved so problematic to Christians, I paid a visit to David Pleins, who teaches in the religious studies department at Santa Clara University in California's Silicon Valley and who has penned a pair of books that explore Darwin's relationship to faith. David's first book on Darwin, called *The Evolving God: Charles Darwin on the Naturalness of Religion* (Bloomsbury Academic, 2013), explores Darwin's lifelong interest in religion. His second book, *In Praise of Darwin: George Romanes and the Evolution of a Darwinian Believer* (Bloomsbury Academic, 2014), explores the overlooked spirituality of George Romanes, a member of Darwin's inner circle, who wrote a long, often sentimental, and deeply pious poem on the occasion of Darwin's death. Both books argue convincingly that neither Charles Darwin nor his closest associates were hostile toward religion.

When I asked David why Darwin's work has caused so much offense among Christians, his answer was quick: "hindsight," he told me, "isn't always 20/20 vision. People tend to ignore and overlook Darwin's religious views. They mistake his personal rejection of religious belief as hostility toward Christianity." In fact—as David points out in his books—Charles

Darwin found religious questions to be both interesting and important. During his voyage on the *Beagle*, Darwin observed and wrote about the religious practices he encountered among the people he visited with the same keen eye for detail he employed while observing and writing about plants and animals, and he reached some of the same conclusions. After observing the pre-Columbian paganism practiced in Tierra del Fuego and comparing it to the Catholicism practiced elsewhere in South America, the Hinduism practiced in Mauritius, and the various forms of Christianity practiced in Europe, he came to believe that humans evolve religiously just as we evolve biologically. That he considered English-style Unitarianism to be the highest form of religious practice betrayed a little bit of colonialist egocentrism, but we'll let it pass.

Darwin's musings on religion—which take up large portions of his personal notebooks—seldom are acknowledged by Darwin's supporters or by his detractors, and thus the religious insights and sensitivities Darwin brought with him to the study of evolution almost never add nuance to the public's understanding of Darwin's scientific contributions. Thus we don't remember that Darwin, though not an orthodox believer himself, wasn't trying to disprove or even to discourage the faith of others. Darwin, it turns out, was someone who didn't feel the need to disparage religious beliefs he did not hold.

"Also," David continued, in answer to my original question about why Darwin has caused such a stir, "Darwin's work speaks to the ways we imagine ourselves, and the implications are huge. They force us to ask who we are as humans." Because Darwin's work at first implied (in *The Origins of Species*) and later explicitly stated (in *The Descent of Man*) that humanity has evolved alongside every other living thing, Darwin's work took humanity off the pedestal upon which Christianity had placed it. If humans evolved like, say, barnacles, then is our status before God any higher than that of the barnacle? Or is the barnacle, like humanity, also made in the image of God?

David went on to explain that these questions arose at a time of turmoil in the religious world, when the established

Anglican Church in England and the Protestant churches of the American establishment were losing both membership and societal influence. Darwin—whether through his work he deserved it or not—became the lynchpin in the debates that arose out of the churches' crisis. Darwinian evolution was not the only subject that divided Christians in the nineteenth century—they also were discussing issues like slavery and the use of modern historical-critical tools for understanding the Bible—but Darwin's theories had a way of catching the attention of people living beyond academia's ivory towers. It was, perhaps, a little easier to imagine—and to be offended by—the idea that one's ancestors looked an awful lot like chimpanzees than it was to make a credible argument in favor of slavery or fully to comprehend the vagaries of the documentary hypothesis.

And so, whereas support for slavery, for the most part, died out in the decades following emancipation (at least in polite society), and whereas strenuous opposition to modern biblical scholarship remains something of a boutique concern, hostility toward Darwin's ideas only has grown alongside an ever more-narrowly literal reading of the Bible. Many of Darwin's earliest critics were "Old Earth Creationists" who studied geological and fossil evidence and came to the conclusion that God created the world in its current form (more or less) a very long time ago, but in the 1960s, beginning, according to David Pleins, with the 1961 publication of a book called *The Genesis Flood: The Biblical Record and Its Scientific Implications* by John C. Whitcomb and Henry M. Morris (Presbyterian and Reformed Publishing, 1961), a more modern, "young earth" creationism became popular among Darwin's dissenters. Young earth creationism—supported by so-called creation science—contends the Bible is a reliable historical and scientific record of the origins of life on earth, which began roughly six thousand years ago.[13]

Since the 1980s those opposed to Darwin's theories have embraced the gentler language and the (seemingly) more reasonable logic of "intelligent design," a rearticulation of arguments for the existence of God that date back to Greek philosophy and that, ironically, find inspiration in the same eighteenth-century scholars of natural theology that inspired Charles Darwin as a student of divinity at Cambridge. The words change and different modes of logic are brought to bear, but the goal is the same: to remove Darwin from his place of prominence among the intellectual giants who guide our understanding of how humans came into existence and what that existence might mean.

This is not the work of thoughtful Christianity. If, as I suggested in the introduction to this book, the practice of thoughtful Christianity begins with being properly informed about matters of faith, then the thoughtful Christian (even and perhaps especially those who read the Bible as science and history) must understand that an embrace of Darwin's theories (and of subsequent ideas about evolution inspired by Darwin) is not a rejection of the Bible or of historical Christianity as practiced by the Church Triumphant since the apostolic age. After all, Christianity existed before Darwin was around to reject, and before Darwin, Christians responded to scientific discovery with varying degrees of acceptance and grace. Thoughtful Christians, being informed by the past, must reach back before Darwin to thinkers like John Calvin, who believed scientific observation was an important tool in the work of understanding the nature of God; and to Origen, who read the Bible as allegory rather than as history; and to countless saints—known and unknown—who have held faith and scientific innovation comfortably together. Then, with a proper understanding of historical Christian thinking, thoughtful Christians may allow their faith to be informed by the contributions of Darwin and by subsequent evolutionary biologists, as well as by other scientific work that has emerged and that will emerge as scientists endeavor to understand the mysteries of creation.

WHERE RELIGION HAPPENS

On the night I stayed in Shrewsbury (which also was my first night on the far side of the Atlantic), as I was preparing to leave my hotel to go out into the rain and find a simple dinner before collapsing in jet-lagged exhaustion into the comfort of my bed, a young man with a violin started talking to me in the hotel lobby, where I was using the establishment's meager Wi-Fi service. My fellow hotel guest was free with suggestions about where I could find a nice dinner in Shrewsbury that wouldn't break the bank, and he invited me to join him and some of his friends later that night at a pub, where he told me the best jam session in all of Shropshire would be taking place. The invitation made me feel a little bit nervous. Part of me still felt like a child who'd been warned never to talk to strangers, and, being a foreigner and not entirely confident socially, I wasn't sure if the violinist inviting me would interpret a visit to the pub as an invitation for romantic overtures (he was, perhaps, a little *too* interested in knowing that we were staying in adjacent hotel rooms).

I went anyway, and I'm glad I did. The pub was tiny, and the room we occupied didn't really hold all of us. The musicians included the aforementioned violinist, three guitarists, a bassist, a mandolin player, a guy on banjo, and a diminutive, somewhat brittle-looking man with a penny whistle; those of us without instruments included the wife and daughter of the banjo player, a tourist couple from somewhere in the south of England who seemed to be in the very springtime of romance, a lonely looking trans-woman, and me. The music ranged from traditional Irish jigs to bluegrass to the Beatles by way of Bob Dylan, Joni Mitchell, and the Delta Blues. Those of us without instruments sang, sometimes managing decent-sounding harmonies.

The musicians were all really talented, and as the evening turned to night, and as we sang song after song, I came to experience deep joy and a sense of belonging born not of nationality or of personal familiarity but of music and of fellowship between people in from the cold and sharing the warmth of a small room heated by a fireplace, bodies, and beer. I have no idea if any of the people with me in the Shrewsbury pub were people of faith, but I do know that religion deals in the currency of such moments, when a beautifully diverse gathering of

God's children come together to make music, to share friendship, and to extend hospitality to strangers.

When yet another musician showed up with a dreadnought guitar, I gave up my seat in the tiny room and walked back through the rain to my hotel. It was 11 p.m. in England, and after a transatlantic flight, I'd been awake for more than thirty hours; I needed sleep. There on the dark, damp streets of an English town I realized that Darwin's detractors don't just misunderstand the science of evolution and they don't just read the Bible in ways it never was meant to be read. They also misunderstand what it means to live a life of faith. Religion's finest moments don't happen when defenders of a relatively modern way of reading the Bible are able to banish evolutionary biology from high school classrooms; rather, religion is at its best when the people of God make music together, singing in such beautiful harmony that they become impatient with all in the world that is ugly, violent, unjust, and unkind. And nothing Darwin—or any other scientist—has done can compromise the Christian faith so long as Christians remember to come in from the cold to sit down by the fire and sing, welcoming the stranger and creating beauty—with all that true beauty means for justice and peace.

To say that religion's finest moments and truest insights happen in the warmth of communities and in experiences of beauty that are in no way threatened by the observations of science is not a saccharine, overly sentimental spirituality. Rather, it is an expression of resistance against those who would make science the foe of faith and scientists the enemies of God, and it frees thoughtful Christians to practice a faith that is formed by truths found in empirical data rendered by the scientific process. For more on what it means to allow empirical data to inform a thoughtful faith, keep reading. It is the subject of the next chapter.

2

Respecting Empirical Data

As an actor I pretend for a living. I play fictitious characters
often solving fictitious problems.

I believe humankind has looked at climate change in that
same way: as if it were a fiction, happening to someone else's
planet, as if pretending that climate change wasn't real would
somehow make it go away.

But I think we know better than that. Every week, we're
seeing new and undeniable climate events, evidence that accelerated climate change is here now. . . . Honored delegates,
leaders of the world, I pretend for a living. But you do not.

—Leonardo DiCaprio, addressing the United Nations
Climate Summit[1]

Whenever Christians talk about the intersection of religion
and science, we are forced to address a question that is perhaps
the most basic philosophical question a person of faith can
(and should) ask: Where do we find the truths that form our
religious worldview? It goes without saying that many of the
truths that shape our devotional inclinations are theological
propositions that are affirmed by faith and that can be neither
proved nor disproved, but what of truth that can be verified
using scientific observations or simple common sense? What
role should empirical data have in shaping who we are as Christians, and what should we do when the stories, theologies, and
values embedded in Christian tradition don't track with information gleaned from the work of scholars and scientists? Must
the claims of faith take primacy over the voice of reason? Must
a thinking person set aside her faith when confronted with
scientific or historical data that challenge conclusions derived
from a literal reading of Holy Writ?

Modern conventional wisdom—as articulated both by religious traditionalists and by atheists—is that when empirical
data and religious claims collide, we must choose between the

two. If, for example, archeologists uncover an 11,000-year-old building in Jericho (which they have[2]), the discovery of which calls into question the biblical claim that the armies of Joshua destroyed *all* of Jericho[3] (to say nothing of the fact that a literal reading of the Bible suggests the world was created five thousand years *after* the construction of the building in question[4]), then conventional wisdom suggests a person of faith is faced with two choices. He can assume (without any supporting evidence) that the archeologists made erroneous deductions about the age of the building or he can reject the Bible.

It is worth asking, however, if such a binary approach to faith and science is reasonable. There is, after all, a third way. It is possible for a person to understand that the Bible is an ancient document written to convey spiritual wisdom rather than historical or scientific fact. As we saw in the last chapter, this reading has been used by great Christian leaders for centuries. It was used by early Church Fathers such as Origen, reformers like John Calvin, and Christians such as Asa Gray, who was among Darwin's staunchest supporters. This third way is a reading of the Bible that makes spiritual space for empirical data and, as such, it has the advantage of denying neither the work of scientists nor the sanctity of Holy Writ, something that recommends it, especially to those wanting to practice a faith capable of being formed by the insights of science and of other scientific pursuits.

To embrace this third way—to affirm a thoughtful faith formed by the work of science—is to practice religion in a way that protects humanity against the tangible threats of ignorance. After all, it is one thing to talk about how archeologists and biblical literalists might have an ideological smackdown over the age of a Neolithic building along the shores of the Dead Sea. It's a debate without much at stake for the disinterested. It is another thing altogether when a rejection of science has serious implications for the health and well-being of the world and of the children of God who call our planet home.

There are plenty of ways to reject solid, scientific information in favor of ideological ignorance. We live in a polarized world in which for every thesis there in an antithesis, even when the original thesis is an easily demonstrated proposition. We divide ourselves into opposing camps: red state/blue state, religious/secular, evangelical/progressive, NASCAR/European soccer, etc., and far too many of us are guilty of allowing these conflicts—rather than empirical data—to define for us what is true. Christians are not alone in our tendency to place political inclination or theological propositions above evidence-based reality, but it would be nice if more often we acted like we know better than to ignore empirical data, especially in matters of great urgency.

REDWOOD SUMMER

During the summer of 1990, in an effort to curtail the logging of old-growth redwood groves, environmental activists from around the world converged in Humboldt and Mendocino counties in Northern California for a season of intense protests, civil disobedience, and direct action against the timber industry. The so-called Redwood Summer was the brain child of organizers affiliated with a radical environmentalist organization, Earth First!, which—like many environmentalist groups—was growing increasingly alarmed by an accelerated harvest of redwoods and by the harm such rapid logging inflicted on the health of the forests and watersheds of Northern California. A call went out and activists responded from all over, passing—by the VW microbus load—into the foggy dampness of California's north coast at the westernmost region of the continental United States.[5]

   To put it mildly, the protests caused division in traditionally timber-industry-reliant communities north of the Redwood Curtain, where jobs harvesting and milling lumber were already threatened by a changing world. The timber industry of Northern California began as a way of supplying lumber to Californian cities whose populations and economies were exploding in the wake of the Gold Rush, but unlike gold

mining—which was relatively short-lived—the timber industry lasted well into the later decades of the twentieth century
thanks to extensive stands of massive trees and to improve-
ments in transportation infrastructure that made the whole
world a market for Californian lumber.

But in the 1980s the industry changed when Houston-based
Maxxam Inc. acquired Pacific Lumber Company—the region's
largest timber company—in a hostile takeover that put Maxxam
$800 million in debt. To pay the debt incurred in the acquisi-
tion of Pacific Lumber Company, Maxxam liquidated Pacific
Lumber Company's relatively generous pension fund, and it
started clear-cutting the forests, a practice other lumber companies in the region soon adopted for themselves.[6] For more
than a century, the timber industry had managed the forests of
Northern California with the goal of sustaining a lumber-based
economy long term. With the arrival of Maxxam, the model
changed to one of extracting massive short-term profits regardless of the effect such practices would have on local economies
or upon the health of the environment.[7]

The steady jobs in the forests and mills that had provided
economic stability in their communities for more than a century were disappearing fast. Now what jobs remained were
facing a new threat, this time from environmentalists, most
of whom wore Birkenstocks and ate granola, who wanted to
halt the harvest of old-growth redwood altogether. For many
loggers and mill workers the arrival of outside protesters felt
like the final straw.

The whole region exploded, and I watched the pyrotechnics
from a front-row seat. I spent that summer directing a small
summer camp owned by a coalition of mostly rural Presbyterian churches in Humboldt County and, along with members
of a local ministerial association, I attended one of the major
protests, which Earth First! organizers staged near a waterfront
paper mill on the Samoa Peninsula across Humboldt Bay from
the city of Eureka. The experience was surreal. On one side
of a police line that included every law-enforcement person
available, including at least one dog catcher (who happened to

belong to one of the Presbyterian congregations that employed me), was a wild assortment of countercultural types yelling and spitting at the cops and demanding an end to the logging of redwood forests. On the other side of the police line were timber industry employees and their family members, who tended to be dressed in steel-toed boots, plaid flannel shirts, and billed caps. They were shouting profanities at their countercultural counterparts, telling them to go home to the city and to stop endangering their jobs.

There was, however an odd twist in the tableaux of protest and counterprotest. As members of the logging community were demanding that their timber industry jobs be preserved, stevedores were loading rough-cut timber onto a large bulk-carrier cargo ship that was docked in Humboldt Bay just behind the counterprotesters. The ship's cargo was bound for Asia, to be milled by folks willing to work for a fraction of what Californian mill workers get paid. And as the environmentalists were protesting the harvest of redwoods, a logging truck drove up, headed to the paper mill. The protesters seized the truck, forcing the driver out of the cab. They then chained themselves in a circle around the truck and its trailer in symbolic defense of the redwoods, except that there wasn't a single redwood log on the truck. It was all tan oak headed to the pulp mill to be turned into paper, and in fact, removing tan oak and other hardwoods is one of the very best things you can do to help redwood forests recover after logging.[8]

I came away from that experience suspecting that the good intentions of those who wanted either to preserve the forest or to save jobs had been hijacked by people who simply wanted to spew invective at those who looked different. People in VW vans wanted to hate the folks in 4x4s and the folks in the pickups were all too happy to return the favor. Had the environmentalists protesting the logging of redwoods been guided by a knowledge of forestry, they would not have commandeered a logging truck filled with tan oak logs; if the loggers and mill workers counterprotesting had been attentive to the easily demonstrable economic data all around them, they would have

joined the environmentalists in protesting the logging companies, whose harvesting and milling practices were doing more
than even the most strident tree-hugging hippie to destroy an
industry that had anchored the region's economy for over a
century.

This is a lesson the thoughtful Christian can—and should—
apply in any number of contemporary debates, not just as a
way of being intellectually honest, but because the health of
the earth and the survival of humanity depend upon the ability of people to make decisions that are guided by empirical
data. The dog pile of animosity I witnessed during Redwood
Summer is not limited to California's north coast, and it did
not dissipate when the protesters left Humboldt County. Such
acrimony is alive and growing today all over the United States;
it is manifested in the ways many of us talk about a wide range
of issues. The animosity is alive when debates about evolution
have more to do with contrasting worldviews (and perhaps the
aesthetics of Bill Nye's bow tie) than with actual, verifiable
information. It's an acrimony seen when arguments about climate change transpire in the context of an American culture
clash in which the drivers of American SUVs and owners of
hybrid automobiles imported from Japan forever are at odds,
often arguing about the relative merits of Fox News rather
than discussing empirical data gleaned from the work of real
scientists.

Many Christians are deep into such arguments; but if Christians want to practice a thoughtful faith we must rise above petty
ideology, choosing instead to engage the world informed—
whenever possible—by what is true. It's not enough simply to
agree with whatever may confirm our preconceived ideas about
faith or our habitual political inclinations; rhetorically thumb-
ing one's nose in the general direction of Houston, Texas, or
Berkeley, California, doesn't do much good. Instead we must
take stock of and learn from those whose scientific explora-
tion has led to that which empirically is true. To suggest that
thoughtful Christians must set aside ideological allegiances in
favor of a faith informed by empirical knowledge is more than

just a call to decent behavior and polite conversations. Rather, it is an acknowledgment that science matters in the real world, where faithful living has a tangible impact.

WHY EVOLUTION MATTERS

When Christians reject Darwin's theories of evolutionary biology, they often do so as a way of defending their faith in what they might call "biblical inerrancy." According to the doctrine of biblical inerrancy, every word in the Bible is reliably true in every possible way. Thus, for those who hold to biblical inerrancy, the Bible—and not science—is the supreme conveyor of empirical information, for the Bible is the final measure of everything real. In an attempt to defend the Bible and to establish Scripture as the ultimate arbiter of truth, local and state lawmakers throughout America have introduced, debated, and passed measures that prohibit—or at least limit—the teaching of evolution in public schools, an issue hardly put to rest by the Scopes trial.

Laws that limit the teaching of evolution are a problem not just because such legislation has the potential to render a population ignorant of basic scientific knowledge but because evolution is an ongoing reality that affects human lives every day. For example, viruses, including Ebola, and bacteria, including drug-resistant tuberculosis, mutate, which is part of the process of their evolution. This makes it difficult to find vaccinations and treatments for the illnesses caused by these pathogens and others like them. Vaccinations against and treatments for illnesses caused by mutating pathogens cannot be developed by those who don't understand the science of evolutionary biology. Thus there are significant—if unintended—public-health implications for a population that refuses to learn from the empirical data rendered by solid science.

Christians who, in deference to the doctrine of biblical inerrancy, reject the empirical data that support the science of evolutionary biology must engage in a high-stakes game of values clarification: For the sake of a better understanding of the work of medicine, should they relent in their opposition to the teaching of evolutionary biology? Or will they embrace a faith with spiritual values that make room for and that are formed, in part, by empirical data?

WHY CLIMATE SCIENCE MATTERS

It is interesting to note that the distrust of science rooted in the Victorian rejection of Darwinism is not limited to evolution. The same Christian suspicion of science that opposes the teaching of evolution also has led to an ambivalence toward listening to the voice of science in the work of caring for creation, particularly in the area of climate change, an endeavor which, necessarily, relies upon scientifically derived empirical data. The Christian tendency to ignore the urgency of earth care is important not because small groups gathered for Bible study in church basements hold contrarian views about climate change. The problem is that several Christians unmoved by scientific data as it relates to earth care in general and climate change in particular are members of the United States Senate and House of Representatives, and as such, they have the capacity to prevent the American government (and the world's largest economy, which produces 17 percent of the world's greenhouse gas emissions) from taking steps necessary to curb global warming.

Despite the fact that some 97 percent of the world's climate scientists agree that humans are responsible for the greenhouse gasses that cause global warming,[9] as I wrote these words in California an action-stalling bloc of Republicans in Washington, DC—56 percent in the U.S. House of Representatives and 65 percent of Republicans in the Senate—were on record denying the existence of human-caused climate change.[10] And while acceptance of climate change science may be more common among non-American world leaders, action is not. In September of 2014—five years after world leaders at a conference in Copenhagen committed to addressing climate change—Oxfam, an international charity that addresses issues of poverty around the globe, released a study that looked at international progress on poverty. Among other things they found that

> more than 650 million people have been affected and more than 112,000 lives lost as a result of weather-related disasters since [the Copenhagen conference in] 2009. Since then, each year has been among the top ten most expensive on record. Poor people are being hit first and hardest by climate change. Many livelihoods and crops have been destroyed, increasing food prices and leaving millions hungry. At the same time, however, international commitments to reverse the threat of climate change have stalled.[11]

It is an unfortunate likelihood that the world's political leaders (especially those who work in Washington) will not take action on climate change unless a well-informed public convinces them to do so. If a thoughtful Christian wishes to be part of a productive, public conversation about caring for the earth—the kind of debate that leads to action that is beneficial—then he or she must come to those conversations guided not by acrimony or even by theological convictions (which on their own cannot move public policy) but by empirical data.

For a thoughtful Christian wanting to form a spiritual practice that involves a deep concern for the earth's changing climate, there is no shortage of empirical data. Scientists studying the earth's climate long have known that human-generated carbon dioxide emissions are trapping heat and creating a greenhouse effect that is causing the average temperature on the earth's surface to warm. The resulting rise in temperature is wreaking a wide range of havoc across the globe: weather patterns are becoming increasingly erratic and dangerous, certain species are becoming extinct, in some places crop yields are diminishing, and the acidity of the ocean water is changing, a development with serious implications for aquatic life.

Perhaps the most alarming result of climate change is melting ice. The two largest repositories of the earth's fresh water supply are the polar ice caps, which are starting to recede. This is no small matter. In Antarctica an entire mountain range roughly the size of the European Alps is buried beneath ice.[12] The melting of such a large amount of ice would be hugely problematic for the more than 1 billion people who live in coastal areas,[13] especially those living in island nations of the Pacific that may be submerged entirely as a result of melting polar ice[14] and those in places like Bangladesh, where 40 percent of the nation's productive land is threatened by rising water.[15] Meanwhile—and perhaps more frighteningly—the melting of glaciers in the Tibetan Plateau threatens the health of rivers that flow from those glaciers and the welfare of the roughly 3 billion people—almost half of the world's population—who live within the rivers' watersheds in ten different countries.[16]

Climate scientists predict a variety of possible endings for the story of climate change, but on this much, nearly every climate scientist agrees: unless humans change our dependence upon carbon-emitting fossil fuels, we're doomed—and even if we *do* change our behavior and rely less upon carbon fuels, it may be too late. We're doomed because climate change has the potential to make the earth profoundly inhospitable to human life, but as bad as the direct effects of climate change likely will end up being, the biggest threat to humanity—as a result of climate change—may be humanity itself. As global temperatures rise, melting polar ice and diminishing Tibetan glaciers will lead to widespread shortages of fresh water, arable land, food, and energy. This scarcity could lead to economic collapse and to armed conflict as nations compete for access to diminishing water and land resources. Three of the nations dependent upon water from the Tibetan plateau possess nuclear weapons, which adds a measure of urgency to the issue of melting ice.

If we are going to embrace a thoughtful faith, then information matters. The gathering of, the interaction with, and the response to empirical data is not just an intellectual amusement for those living in ivory towers, surrounded by the musty smell of books. It is an exercise with deep moral implications. To ignore demonstrable facts is to put very real human lives at risk.

If, as people of faith, we want to be part of reversing—or even of mitigating—the pace of climate change, then we will need to be well-informed so that we can make choices grounded in the best, most up-to-date information on offer from the scientific community.

BUT HOW DO WE KNOW?

There is a problem, of course, and that is that few thoughtful people—Christian or otherwise—have the capacity to evaluate primary empirical data relating to evolutionary biology or climate change. Most of us aren't research scientists with a knowledge of fossils or access to the equipment necessary to measure global temperatures or the levels of carbon dioxide in the atmosphere. In fact, most of us aren't even able properly to interact with empirical data by reading and by understanding the findings of biologists or climatologists as they are recorded in scientific journals. Scientific writing is too technical, and so we rely on journalists and pundits who communicate—often erroneously—the work of science to a broader public. As a result, much of what most of us know about evolution and climate change comes to us three or four times removed from original data, which makes it hard to know which information is reliable and which is not.

In sorting through questions about reliable data it helps to know a scientist. It's especially helpful if you are a pastor and the scientist you know is an elder in your church, and she is willing to chat over a cup of coffee and to talk about how empirical data can form faith. Cynthia Cudaback—the scientist in question—holds degrees from the University of California at Berkeley (BS with honors in physics) and the University of Washington, where she earned a PhD in geophysics. She has held teaching positions at the University of California at Santa Barbara and North Carolina State University. She is the daughter of an astronomer and the wife of a scientist who studies the earth's electromagnetic polarity. Science permeates everything she does. I asked her how a nonscientist like me could differentiate between reliable empirical data rendered by the dispassionate filtration of the scientific method and the work of those more interested in the promotion of ideologies (such as biblical inerrancy) or industries (such as the petrochemical industry, which has much to lose should the world's economies choose to fight global warming by cutting carbon emissions). She acknowledged it is a problem.

"Unfortunately, there's no way empirically to create space for empiricism," she told me. "We can't describe why science works," she said while discussing the ability of the scientific method to render empirical data that help us understand the world. "All we can do is observe that science *does* work, but even so, what we believe about the value of science usually has more to do with our identity than it does with what we have actually learned from science."

People supported the science that fueled the space race, for example, because sending people to the moon was a "sexy" idea ("and very masculine, with all those rockets," Cynthia notes). Reducing our collective carbon footprint just isn't as sexy a cause. Part of the problem may be that technological innovation on the scale of a space race isn't even needed to reduce human emissions of greenhouse gasses. "We don't even really need to convert to solar and wind power or drive electric cars— although those things are great," Cynthia told me. "What we need to do is reorganize our society. We need to live in smaller, more walkable communities. We need better public transportation. We need to consume less and be more efficient. It's not rocket science—but again, I think that's the problem."

When it comes to the question of evolution, persons of faith freed from the need to self-identify as biblical literalists and willing to listen to the voice of science no longer are required to worship a God who, in Cynthia's words, "messes with your brains" by creating a universe that, upon the closer observations of science, does not look like the cosmos described in Genesis. "The intellectual contortions a person has to go through to believe the words of Genesis are scientifically valid strike me as humiliating," she confided, "and the same goes for those who deny the science of climate change. The scientific evidence is overwhelming, but for far too many people, climate change denial is an identity that has more to do with politics and socioeconomic factors than it has to do with empirical data."

The good news is that such identities can change as our spiritual lives mature and as we grow in thoughtfulness, and here I speak from personal experience. When I was in high school I was convinced my life's work would—in some way—include the task of dismantling the formidable edifice of empirical data that had been constructed by (at the time) a century of evolutionary biology. My grasp of the rudiments of high school biology wasn't sufficient to help me see the folly of my ambitions, but during the last semester of my senior year in high school I took a geology class, and for the first time I truly understood how empirical data can serve as a springboard from which to dive into the deep waters of knowledge. What I was learning—that the earth was much older than a strict reading of the Bible suggests, and that the evolution of species is, indeed, recorded in fossil evidence, despite Genesis's suggestion that every living thing sprang into being in its current form—caused me to doubt not just the Bible but the very existence of the God whose reality was, for me, overly dependent upon a fairly narrow reading of the Old Testament.

What saved my faith was an academic study of the Old Testament, which began later that year during my first semester at Westmont College in Santa Barbara, California. In my Old Testament class the professor presented the book of Genesis, with its creation narratives, its flood story, and its accounts of the lives of spiritual ancestors, not as science or as history but as a collection of ancient Near-Eastern myths. This is not to say the stories of Genesis are untrue; rather, it is to say that their truth is found in spiritual meaning and not in provable scientific fact.

There was nothing new in the way of reading the Bible presented to me in the first semester of my college experience. As mentioned at the beginning of this chapter, it is a method for reading the Bible employed by many great saints, but for me it was revolutionary. Toward the end of my first semester in college I found a field of fossilized seashells while hiking in the hills above Santa Barbara and I realized that the fossils no longer were a threat to my faith. I didn't have to pretend it made sense to believe they'd been deposited several hundred feet above sea level by a flood in the days of Noah. Rather, without disrespecting the Bible, I was freed to accept what I knew scientifically to be true: that the hills upon which I was hiking once had been under the ocean but had been pushed up over millions of years as continental plates collided, a process that is ongoing and that is experienced and can be observed every time there is an earthquake in California.

My moment of enlightenment was possible not just because I'd been exposed to what empirical data reveal about the formation of the earth's landscapes but also because I'd learned some important empirical data about the Bible: that many of the stories in Genesis thematically and stylistically are similar to other ancient Near-Eastern myths and that the first chapter of Genesis describes not the world we observe today, but the universe as it was understood by ancient Mesopotamian cultures.[17]

Empirical data aren't always important (any fan of the San Francisco Giants will consider the Los Angeles Dodgers to be a subpar baseball team, even when the Dodgers beat the Giants 17 to 0 at home during a pennant race[18]), but to practice a thoughtful faith that is informed by what is measurable and demonstrable is to join forces with those of every faith (and none) whose practical, rational, and fact-based ideas and solutions have the potential to heal the world by saving us from our ignorance.

To allow one's faith to be formed by empirical data is not to surrender one's spirituality to nefarious secular forces dedicated to the work of discrediting the historical claims of the Christian faith; nor is it necessary to reject the Bible if one wants to embrace knowledge born of scientifically sound information. Rather, to practice a faith formed by empirical data is to be religious in a way that makes sense. It is to live a life in which spiritual wisdom dovetails nicely with more terrestrial knowledge and in which both ways of knowing inform and support each other. To live thus is to practice a thoughtful faith.

3

Wrestling with Tradition

Knowledge puffs up, but love builds up.
—St. Paul, 1 Corinthians 8:1

That being said, if one wishes to be a thoughtful Christian, scientific discovery and empirical knowledge are not enough. For the urgent and often complicated work of making the world a better, more peaceful place, a thoughtful Christian must engage the traditions of our faith which, through a process of historical trial and error, give us guidance as we attempt to follow Jesus—in word and in deed—by declaring the nearness of God's kingdom of peace.

However indispensible they may be, facts, figures, and rational explanations do not make us better people. They do not inspire charity, nor do they create beauty. The strong American emphasis on and investment in STEM (science, technology, engineering, and math) education has not kept our society peaceable, just, equitable, or able to demonstrate much evidence that we care about the health of the world's biodiversity, the purity of the earth's air, the productivity of its soil, or the cleanliness of its water.

From the last hundred years of human history we see that science, unguided by a moral compass, has led to such technology as could destroy the lives of every human on the planet with a presidential push of a button and the launch of a nuclear war. Engineering, unmoved by awe in the face of creation's beauty, has despoiled places of great natural wonder in search of fossil fuels, the burning of which is causing the temperature of the earth's atmosphere to rise catastrophically. Mathematics unfettered from the constraints of social justice has been used to create a system of international banking that has consolidated the world's financial wealth in the offshore bank accounts belonging to a tiny fraction of the world's individuals and corporations. Currently, the United States produces more STEM PhDs than any country save China,[1] yet all that knowledge has not prevented us from being a nation constantly at war, it has not preserved the environment, and it has not maintained economic equity among our citizens.

For instruction on how to be better people and how to create societies that are just and nations that are peaceful, we must turn to religious and ethical traditions, which is problematic because humans have been exploring religious and ethical concepts for far longer than they have been pursuing empirical knowledge. In our aspirations for a more just, equitable, and peaceable world, our spiritual knowledge has helped us even less than our academic knowledge. Yet dismissing meaningful and thoughtful interactions with religious and ethical traditions as unimportant because of their failure to yield positive results is like setting aside the study of climate science due to its seeming inability to apply brakes on the runaway train of global warming.

This is why we cannot simply learn our traditions, but also must interact with them thoughtfully. Just as a knowledge of climate science offers solutions to help curb the effects of climate change, so also a faithful and thoughtful interaction with religious and ethical traditions has the potential to mitigate the consequences of humanity's seeming inability to refrain from violence. Just as a knowledge of climate science has inspired individuals, communities, and nations to seek alternatives to fossil fuels, so also a thoughtful consideration of religious and ethical traditions has the potential to enable humans to choose nonviolence over armed conflict, charity over greed, and social justice over institutional avarice.

SANTIAGO DE COMPOSTELA AND THE PROBLEM OF CHRISTIAN VIOLENCE

We cannot simply accept religious tradition without thoughtful consideration because every religion I know about is composed of a mix of traditions, many of them wonderfully nurturing and beautifully peaceful, and others violent and repressive. Christianity is no exception. To say that the theological traditions of the Christian faith send mixed messages is an understatement. Far too often the Church's spirituality, theology, and liturgy have been formed by violence, fear, hatred, and greed—but not always. Much of our Christian heritage is beautiful, delightful, and powerful in its demand for social justice and peace, and to the thoughtful Christian falls the job of judging between what is noxious and what is wonderful so that we can bring to prominence all within our faith that is good and honorable and beautiful and true.

Nowhere are the conflicting messages in the Christian tradition more stark than in its relationship to violence, and nowhere is Christianity's mixed message on violence more powerfully contrasted than in Santiago de Compostela in the Spanish region of Galicia, on the northwest corner of the Iberian peninsula. The proper way to travel to Santiago de Compostela is by foot. For more than a thousand years, pilgrims have made their way to the city in Galicia, walking from various parts of Western Europe to visit the shrine of Santiago Matamoros, or in English, "St. James, the Killer of Moors," the killed in question being the Muslims who, for seven centuries, dominated various parts of southern Spain.

According to tradition, in the year 813, a hermit named Pelayo had a vision of strange lights and heavenly music near the ruins of an old Roman fortress named Campus Stellae, which means "field of stars," and from which is derived the name "Compostela." Pelayo reported his vision to a local bishop, who made his way to the place of the vision and determined it to be the resting place of the earthly remains of St. James, the son of Alpheus, the brother of John the Evangelist, and a member of Jesus' inner circle.

Legends tell us St. James traveled to the Iberian peninsula as a missionary in faithfulness to Jesus' Great Commission to take the gospel to the ends of the earth (which at the time would have been the Atlantic coast of the Iberian peninsula, at least for those living in the Mediterranean world; in fact the Romans named the part of the Galician coast just beyond Santiago *Finis Terrae—Finisterre*, in Spanish—which means "end of the earth"), but the stories tell us that James found his missionary work in Spain to be difficult. The Blessed Virgin (who at the time was still very much alive on the other side of the Mediterranean sea) appeared to James, standing on a pillar, and assured the struggling evangelist that all would be well. It didn't help much. Before too long James went home to Palestine, where Herod Agrippa martyred the pilgrim apostle in the year 44.

For reasons that are not entirely clear, after his death, James's friends decided to send his remains back to Spain, a place James didn't really like all that much. Some versions of the legend say a boat made of marble conveyed James's body to the end of the known world by sailing itself across the Mediterranean, through the Strait of Gibraltar, north past modern-day Portugal, and then up the rivers of Galicia to the place that would become Santiago de Compostela. The legends say locals were impressed to the point of conversion by the arrival of the saint's earthly remains, which a pair of formerly cantankerous, untrainable, and almost certainly pagan bulls conveyed from the magical boat on the riverbank to their final resting place, where they've been ever since.

Nonetheless, the stories report that before too long the locals more or less forgot about the saint's miraculous arrival, and they neglected his tomb. All memory of the pilgrim saint faded and his shrine crumbled, a victim of time, moss, and lichen (which, in Galicia, is as ubiquitous as the wind and rain), only to be rediscovered centuries later when the shepherd Pelayo saw a heavenly vision and led a local bishop to the apostle's tomb. When news of the discovery of the relics of St. James reached King Alfonso II of Asturias and Galicia, the devout monarch built a basilica in which to house the saint's relics. The church was dedicated in 893, and, almost immediately, Santiago became a place of pilgrimage.

As a medieval city with a mythical claim to be the resting place of an important saint, Santiago was not unique. Pilgrimage was an important part of Christian spiritual practice in the Middle Ages,[2] and those cities able, with some validity, to establish themselves as a spiritual destination were in a position to turn religious devotion into a profitable business. At the same time Santiago de Compostela began to welcome pilgrims, churches and cities across Europe were establishing shrines and building cathedrals to house them. What set Santiago apart was its eventual connection to the spirituality of the crusades, especially to those "holy" wars fought by Christians against Islam, both in the Holy Land and, more importantly, in Southern Spain where, in 711 CE, Muslims established a succession of kingdoms after defeating the Visigoths, who ruled the southern parts of the Iberian Peninsula after conquering it from the Roman Empire.

To this day, many of the images of St. James to be found in Santiago de Compostela depict the apostle as a pilgrim—a spiritual wanderer known by his wide-brimmed hat, his walking stick, and his drinking gourd. He is a saint in search of holiness and a simple life, a fellow traveler who welcomes the penitent and those in search of a deeper connection to God. Yet alongside these images of the mendicant apostle are images of Santiago Matamoros, the slayer of Muslims, a ferocious fighter astride a powerful warhorse wielding a nasty-looking sword, which he uses to hack away at the Muslims his horse is trampling. The only thing connecting the pilgrim saint and Matamoros is that both versions of the apostle wear the wide-brimmed hat. Santiago is a place of competing spiritual modalities that must be sorted out thoughtfully.

No one knows for sure when St. James the Pilgrim (whose lifetime predates the founding of Islam by six hundred years) became associated with the holy slaughter of Muslims, but a legend, which appears to have originated in the twelfth century, tells the story of St. James appearing in the guise of a handsome knight on horseback, inspiring the Christian warriors from northern Spain to claim an improbable victory against Muslims from Córdoba.

However fictional the visions of St. James may have been, by 997, the cult of St. James was important enough that it caught the attention of the Córdoban military leader, Al-Mansur, who sacked Santiago de Compostela and stole the cathedral bells, which he converted to lamps for the illumination of the Córdoba mosque. Al-Mansur's victory was humiliating for Spain's northern kingdoms, but it also provided a rallying point for Spanish Christians. It elevated the shrine of St. James in Santiago from a place of local devotion to a place of international pilgrimage, and Europe's preeminent place of inspiration for the soldiers of Christ,[3] who invoked St. James in prayer before engaging Muslims in battle.[4] So strong was Santiago's association with holy war that even the legend of Pelayo's vision and participation in the subsequent discovery of the saint began to feel too peaceable. In the twelfth century, stories attributing the discovery of the tomb to Charlemagne, the great Christian warrior-king who once defeated the armies of the Umayyad Emir of Córdoba in Spain, began to compete with Pelayo's older (if equally mythic) legends.

Eventually Santiago de Compostela became the most important pilgrimage destination in Europe, as hundreds of thousands of pilgrims throughout the Middle Ages walked from across Europe to pray at the shrine of a pilgrim saint who, at some point, became an icon of and an inspiration for unspeakable acts of religious violence.[5]

The closest I got to walking the pilgrimage trail was the trek from Santiago's train station, by way of a nice lunch, to the massive and ornate cathedral. A Calvinist has no words for the kind of ecclesiastical appointments that adorn the high altar in the basilica of Santiago de Compostela. Everything that isn't made of gold seems to be made of some kind of precious gemstone. The focal point of the altar is a massive statue of Saint James, depicted as a pilgrim, except no pilgrim ever wore such finery. (Millions of pilgrims have experienced the feeling of this finery, however, as part of the pilgrim itinerary involves climbing into the altar to embrace the statue from behind.) Above the statue of St. James the Pilgrim, four of what must be the largest cherubs in heaven or on earth hold aloft a statue of Santiago Matamoros riding his white stallion and slaughtering Muslims while statues of several of Spain's greatest kings pay him homage.

In the cathedral, images of St. James the Pilgrim outnumber images of Matamoros, but the slayer of Moors is given the place of highest honor. This celebration of violence doesn't always sit easily with the modern keepers of the basilica. One of the cathedral's side chapels features a large and particularly gruesome depiction of Santiago Matamoros seated, as always, on his white stallion with a drawn sword ready to slaughter the Muslims being trampled by his steed. The smiling busts of Popes John Paul II and Benedict XIV gaze approvingly from a niche above the depiction of the apostle killing Arabs, but when I visited, the carnage was hard to see. Someone had covered the images of dying and suffering Arabs with a huge spray of flowers that betrayed the hidden violence as they wilted.

In Santiago there is no avoiding the presence of Matamoros. His emblem—that of a red crusader's cross modified to look like a sword—is ubiquitous in Santiago. It is worn by pilgrims and it is sold in gift shops, available as earrings, letter openers, and bookmarks. Santiago de Compostela is a place where the spirituality of the Crusades, though somewhat sublimated, still abides.

And almost no one talks about it. Few Christian commentators have spoken out against the violent spirituality of the place that historically has been, after Rome, Western Christianity's second holiest city and that is, after Rome and Jerusalem, the third most popular destination for Christian pilgrims of every denomination to this day. If such a monument to faith-based slaughter existed in Medina or Tel Aviv, Christians would not delay in finding eloquently strenuous articulations of the need for "moderate" Muslims and Jews to condemn the violence inherent in their respective traditions, yet among the followers of Jesus, few thoughtful voices have risen up to condemn Santiago's celebration of slaughter carried out under the sign of the cross.

CRUSADER SPIRITUALITY, ANCIENT AND MODERN

It's hard not to suspect that Christian silence in the face of Santiago's blatant violence may have something to do with the fact that violent images and ideas are so pervasive in Christian spirituality that we have become immune to the shock such images and ideas may otherwise inspire among moral and decent human beings. Ours is a violent Bible, filled with stories of wholesale slaughter and laws that countenance rape and that require capital punishment for gay men and for children who sass their parents. At least one of the Bible's poems wistfully imagines the blessed happiness of those privileged to dash the heads of Babylonian children against rocks.[6] Many Christians worship a God who demands the blood of his Only Son as satisfaction for his otherwise unquenchable rage and who sends those not bathed in the divine bodily fluids into an eternity of suffering and torment.

It was not always thus, however, and for Christians who want also to maintain a spiritual connection to the faith of their foremothers and fathers but who are reluctant to endorse the violent traditions of the historical Church, there is the option of making a thoughtful embrace of Christianity's peaceable traditions. Many of the earliest Christians were pacifists (more about that later), and ideas about God demanding Christ's blood as a satisfaction for his wrath didn't arise until about the same time peaceful images of St. James as a pilgrim saint were starting to be replaced by images of Santiago Matamoros.

The Christian shift toward an embrace of violence began in the fourth century of the Common Era, when Constantine was the first Roman emperor to wage battle under the sign of the cross. As Christianity increasingly became associated with the power of empires and kingdoms, the faith that originally pledged fidelity to the prince of peace became more warlike.

At various times and places between the fourth and the eleventh centuries, Christians marched into war under the banner of the cross, often with the encouragement and the approval of the church, but in 1095 the nature of Christian holy war changed—and the course of Western civilization with it—when Pope Urban II, at the behest of the Byzantine emperor, called upon European Christians to muster for war. He promised plenary indulgence—the complete forgiveness of sins—to anyone willing to join in the fight to liberate Jerusalem from the Seljuk Turks who, early in the eleventh century, conquered the Holy City and who, unlike their Fatimid, Abbysid, and Ummayad Muslim predecessors, restricted Christian access to Jerusalem's holy sites, including the Church of the Holy Sepulcher, the place traditionally associated with Jesus' death and resurrection.

Thus began the Crusades, a word that, when used with a capital "C," refers to wars fought against Muslims in the Holy Land; the Roman Catholic Church also called for crusades (lowercase "c") against the Cathars in the south of France (a war that lasted most of the thirteenth century) and against the Muslim kingdoms and caliphates in southern Spain—a set of wars that lasted from the eighth century until 1492, at which point the crusaders went on to conquer much of the New World, also with the approval and active participation of the Church.[7]

Modern apologists for the Crusades (and other crusades) sometimes suggest that the holy wars waged by Christendom against Islam in the Middle East and Spain and against heretics in the south of France were not really religious in their motivation but were, in fact, the kind of conflicts that might be expected in the push and pull between great political powers. According to this revisionist narrative, the crusaders themselves were motivated by the acquisition of power and the spoils of war more than by any kind of deep spirituality.[8] There is some truth to such apologia, but they tend to put the temporal cart before the spiritual horse.

It is true that the Crusades (and the crusades) occasionally were lucrative business, and to those military leaders able to conquer territory also went the power associated with controlling large swaths of real estate, but for most crusaders holy war was a financial disaster.[9] However much wealth and power may have inspired some individuals to participate in holy war, there is little doubt that the chief impulse behind the Crusades (and the crusades) was spiritual. When the shrine to St. James in Santiago de Compostela was desecrated by Muslims from Córdoba, and more significantly, when the Church of the Holy Sepulcher, the greatest pilgrimage destination of them all, was closed down to Christian visitors, it provoked war that was considered a spiritual duty.

The broad impact of the crusading spirituality should not be underestimated. Writing with a cultural naïveté typical of a mid-twentieth century, Eurocentric worldview, the Russian French novelist and medieval scholar Zoé Oldenbourg wrote,

> Whatever one means by the word, there is no doubt that the early Crusades gave rise to a particular concept of the glory which belongs specifically to the Latin West, and which consequently contributed more than a little to the formation of that European civilization which, in our own time, has finally come to mean civilization itself.[10]

AMERICAN PROTESTANT CRUSADER MENTALITY

In American Protestant churches the spirituality of holy war rooted in the Crusades and so readily apparent in Santiago is preserved in hymnody. If one remembers that medieval crusaders fought under the sign of the cross, it's hard to avoid the faith-based violence inherent in many of Protestantism's favorite hymns. In less than five minutes, without immediate access to the internet or a hymnal, my wife and I were able to recall the following stanzas from hymns we've memorized:[11]

> Onward, Christian soldiers
> Marching as to war,
> With the cross of Jesus
> Going on before!

and

> Stand up, stand up for Jesus,
> Ye soldiers of the cross

and

> Lead on, O King eternal,
> the day of march has come;
> henceforth in fields of conquest
> your tents will be our home.
> Through days of preparation
> your grace has made us strong;
> and now, O King eternal,
> we lift our battle song.

and

> Thou wast their Rock,
> their Fortress, and their Might;
> Thou, Lord, their Captain
> in the well-fought fight;
> Thou, in the darkness drear,
> their one true Light.
> Alleluia.[12]

It is said that what's bred in the bone will come out in the flesh. The violence bred in Christendom's bones after centuries of faith formed by the spirituality of holy war that cuts across centuries, transcends denominational differentiation, and is celebrated in liturgy and hymn—this violence has indeed come out in the flesh of contemporary modes of Christian practice that remain silent in the face of fairly blatant religiously motivated violence.

During the First Gulf War, in speeches before Congress and in remarks broadcast to the nation on television, President

George H. W. Bush justified the American use of armed force to expel Iraq from Kuwait by using religious language that juxtaposed the evil of Iraqi president Saddam Hussein with America's commitment to morality, decency, and love of peace.[13] In less public spaces, the president was more direct in his insistence that American violence in the Middle East bore the imprimatur of the Divine. Speaking at the National Prayer Breakfast—a gathering of the American evangelical political and economic elite[14]—during the height of Operation Desert Storm, Bush said,

> You know, America is a nation founded under God. And from our very beginnings we have relied upon His strength and guidance in war and in peace. . . . I have learned what I suppose every President has learned, and that is that one cannot be President of our country without faith in God and without knowing with certainty that we are one nation under God. . . . we must trust Him and keep faith in Him.
>
> And so, we ask His blessings upon us and upon every member not just of our Armed Forces but of our coalition armed forces, with respect for the religious diversity that is represented as these 28 countries stand up against aggression.
>
> Today I'm asking and designating that Sunday, February 3rd, be a national day of prayer. And I encourage all people of faith to say a special prayer on that day—a prayer for peace, a prayer for the safety of our troops, a prayer for their families, a prayer for the innocents caught up in this war, and a prayer that God will continue to bless the United States of America.[15]

While American mainline Protestant churches, for the most part, condemned the use of violence to resolve the conflict in the Middle East (evidence that many thoughtful Christians do, in fact, eschew violence),[16] the largest American Christian groups—the Roman Catholic Church, the National Association of evangelicals, and the Southern Baptist Convention—all were either noncommittal or supportive of the war,[17] and Billy Graham, arguably the nation's most prominent religious leader, spent the night at the White House, supporting the president on the night the war began.[18]

Two presidential administrations later, when the second President Bush proposed a war against Iraq, his biggest supporters were evangelical Christians,[19] many of whom framed the war—despite presidential protestations to the contrary—as a latter-day Crusade, an apocalyptic conflict between Christianity and Islam. Such an embrace of the spirituality of *Matamoros* might be expected on the fringes of the religious right or on some of the internet's wackier websites, but the idea that Islam somehow is connected to the Antichrist and that Christians are virtuous to oppose Muslims with such force reaches well into the mainstream. Televangelist Pat Robertson has called upon Christians to stand up to Islam in the same way they stood up to Nazism,[20] and the dubiously self-proclaimed "former terrorist" Walid Shoebat has called Islam the Antichrist and has praised Russia for its willingness to seek and to receive the blessings of the Orthodox Church as it prepares to do battle against Islam.[21]

A person could be forgiven for counting Robertson and Shoebat among the ranks of the fringe—and indeed their ideas tend to be somewhat offbeat—but Robertson runs a huge media empire, and Shoebat, at U.S. taxpayer expense under the auspices of the Department of Homeland Security, has preached his crusading message to a wide variety of law enforcement agencies[22] and military personnel.[23] Such efforts are helping to transform the United States' military—the most powerful fighting force in human history—from a largely secular force dedicated to the protection of a free democracy to a body of warriors who conflate spiritual and earthly battles and who, like the cross-bearing crusaders in the past, see the destruction of Islam as part of their calling and destiny.[24]

A LONG TRADITION OF CHRISTIAN PACIFISM

While listening to the violent ostinato in the symphony of Christian history, it can be tempting to allow bloodshed and war to define both what Christianity has been for two millennia and what it will become. And to be sure, a judgment of Christianity based solely on empirical evidence must conclude that over the years Christians have, in fulfillment of Jesus' stern warnings, lived by the sword and, as often as not, died by the sword as well. But an analysis based in fact also requires us to acknowledge that Santiago Matamoros, the slayer of Muslims, is not the only icon of traditional Christian attitudes toward war. Also present in the collective Christian spiritual database of guiding images is that of Santiago *Peligrino*, the pilgrim, who invites Christians to join him on a spiritual journey toward peace. What purely empirical knowledge cannot do is instruct the faithful about which avatar is a better representation of what is best in Christianity and which avatar is better for the health of the world. For that higher task, that more urgent and important judgment, Christians must engage in a thoughtful interaction with the various, often competing traditions of faith.

During the early years of the Christian faith—the so-called patristic era between Jesus and Constantine that lasted a little less than three hundred years—many of the Church Fathers taught Christians to shun military service and the warfare that attends it. Tertullian (c. 160–c. 225)—who sometimes is called the Father of Latin Theology—was opposed to Christians serving as soldiers. This opposition, for the most part, had to do with the requirement that Roman soldiers pay tribute to pagan gods, but Tertullian also had concerns about the violence inherent to military service:

> Shall it be lawful for [a Christian] to deal with the sword, when the Lord declareth that "he that useth the sword shall perish by the sword"? And shall the *son of peace* act in battle, whom it will not befit even to *go to law?* Shall he administer bonds and imprisonment, and tortures, and punishments, who may not *avenge* even his own injuries?[25]

Origen of Alexandria (184–253) argued that the Christian's patriotic duty was to be rendered spiritually rather than militarily.

> We do, when occasion requires, give help to kings, and that, so to say, a divine help, "putting on the whole armour of God." And this we do in obedience to the injunction of the

apostle, "I exhort, therefore, that first of all, supplications, prayers, intercessions, and giving of thanks, be made for all men; for kings, and for all that are in authority;" and the more any one excels in piety, the more effective help does he render to kings, even more than is given by soldiers, who go forth to fight and slay as many of the enemy as they can.[26]

Admittedly, the early Christian commitment to pacifism often had less to do with an opposition to the idea of warfare than with the idea of pledging one's allegiance to a pagan king and to his gods, and when Constantine and subsequent Roman emperors began first to decriminalize and then to embrace Christianity, the Church set aside pacifism in favor of principles for fighting "just" wars. Writing at a time when the Church was transitioning into its role as official religion of the empire, Augustine of Hippo—perhaps the greatest theologian of his era (and some would argue of any era)—despised war but suggested that war could be just and that wise persons could fight in just wars.[27] Centuries later, Thomas Aquinas relied upon Augustine in the development of his criteria for waging a just war: it must be declared by a legitimate power, it must be waged for a just cause, with just aims, and with peace as the ultimate goal; clergy cannot be combatants, and ambushing the enemy is fine.[28]

During the Reformation, some of Protestantism's more radical expressions—such as the Anabaptists (see chap. 6) and the Quakers—adopted a strict practice of pacifism, but for the most part the Reformers reaffirmed older notions of just war with varying degrees of strictness. Huldrych Zwingli, for example, died in battle, while John Calvin, in a sermon on Deuteronomy 20:16–20, wrote,

> Though [God] permits us to kill people, he still wants us to exercise humanity . . . Let us note, therefore that wars are never so permissible that they can be allowed to destroy everything and create utter confusion. And we must remember that however much we exercise restraint, the damage done will still be too great. When even one person

is killed it is, alas, an image of God that is destroyed. And when great numbers are killed, there will be many widows and orphans; and even if goods and possessions are spared, many people will be displaced from their homes and badly treated, so that some will die of cold and some of other ills. So, even if we behave as fairly as possible in time of war there will inevitably be many evils. All the more reason, therefore, to refrain from doing wrong and avoid cruelty of any kind.[29]

In the pacifism of the early Church, in the various views on just war held by Augustine, Aquinas, and Calvin, and in the strict nonviolence of the Anabaptists there is a wide range of opinion regarding the intersection of faith and violence, but all of these traditions stand in opposition to the spirit of Santiago Matamoros, whose image inspires not so much just war as murder in the name of God and territorial conquest that expands the boundaries of Christendom with the edge of a sword rather than by the force of the gospel. To journey through life along paths that avoid violence altogether or to travel along the ridgeline that separates the watersheds of war and peace is to follow the way of Saint James the Pilgrim. This is the path of the thoughtful Christian.

VIOLENCE IN THE MODERN WORLD

Ours is an era of wars and rumors of war. I wrote this chapter during the summer that marked the one hundredth anniversary of the outbreak of World War I. That "War to End All Wars" ended up being the opening act[30] in a violent drama that would last a century and that is ongoing today. As one world war gave rise to another, and as the Second World War left the planet riven by a "cold" war that wasn't so cold in places like Iraq, Afghanistan, and El Salvador (to say nothing of Vietnam and Angola), it also set the stage for today's conflicts in the Middle East (where the United States now is embroiled in the mess created when it overthrew the regime of Saddam Hussein, its former Cold War ally), in Central Asia (where, as of this writing, the United States had spent thirteen years fighting the Afghani Taliban, an enemy we once supplied with weapons and money back when they called themselves the mujahideen and were fighting our Cold War nemesis, the Soviet Union), and in Central America (where decades of Cold War-era conflict have left the region impoverished and in the grip of ongoing violence).

A thoughtful assessment of the last century's worth of violence may lead to the observation that, for the most part, war cultivates more war. The flower of peace does not grow in soil that has been watered with blood, and yet Santiago Matamoros rides forth on his warhorse. His sword is held aloft, looking for its next victims, and a lot of Christians are following him, waving national flags and lifting high the cross, as if fighting under the emblem of faith is a sure way to win heaven's favor.

St. James the Pilgrim also is on the move. As always, he is in search of a deeper connection to the divine, and he journeys along a more peaceful path. His entourage is not so well-organized or flashy as that of his warring counterpart. His are the advantages of faithfulness and of hope for a better future, and we can join his company when, after thoughtful interactions with the Christian tradition, we learn that his footsteps—though wandering and sometimes unsure—fall in closer to the way of Christ than does the cadence of legions of soldiers marching to war under the emblem of the cross. To the thoughtful Christian goes a choice: Will we march with Santiago Matamoros or walk with St. James the Pilgrim?

TAKING LEAVE OF MATAMOROS

When it was time to leave Santiago de Compostela, to make my way back to California, I decided to return one last time to the basilica, to honor Santiago Peligrino, the pilgrim saint whose image looms above the high altar, there to be embraced by peaceful pilgrims. After attending a mass at which music from the basilica's massive organ rang through the transept and nave, I climbed up the stairs behind the altar to bid goodbye to the saint, and as I was preparing to embrace him as had millions of pilgrims before me, I noticed his cape, a garment made of sliver and gemstones that must be changed every five hundred years or so due to the corrosive effects of the oil on pilgrims' hands. The current cape, which dates back to the nineteenth century, is covered with cannons and military snare drums. In Santiago, even the pilgrim saint has been drafted into military service.

Jesus once said that peacemakers are numbered among the children of God and that the meek would inherit the earth. I trust these beatitudes will prove true in the Kingdom of God, but in the meantime, at least in Santiago de Compostela, the violent and proud pay the bills, and it is their spirituality that reigns supreme.

But if we practice a thoughtful faith, that needn't be true for us.

PART II

The Marks of a Thoughtful Faith

4

Learning from What Is Old

[The Bible is the] ultimate immigration handbook.
—Samuel Kobia, former General Secretary,
World Council of Churches[1]

There are times, however, when an appeal to Christian tradition isn't enough. When interacting with tradition, the thoughtful Christian enters into historical and theological debates that, while often rich in their potential for spiritual nourishment and intellectual invigoration, can be insufficient for addressing urgent issues that require an immediate response. In times of crisis when public morality ebbs and the waters of justice recede, when the exposed rocks and reefs of societal sin threaten to sink the meager and often beleaguered vessel of social righteousness, then it becomes necessary for thoughtful Christians to employ the millennia-old language of prophecy—to speak on God's behalf using the primordial vocabulary of Scripture that calls us to repent, that confronts complacency, and that has the power to guide us through treacherous seas into a safe harbor of justice and peace.

Most of us, upon surveying the history of the Christian Church, are most proud to call ourselves Christians and to claim an allegiance to the Church when we remember times in which thoughtful Christians have employed biblical prophetic language to address societal evil. Most of us are happy to remember the ways in which Christians spoke out against the institution of slavery. We are eager to identify ourselves with the Confessing Church movement in Germany, which spoke out against the evils of the Third Reich even before the advent of the Holocaust. We are proud to know that the American civil rights movement was born in the Church and that its most eloquent and powerful leader was a man of the cloth; similarly we are happy to embrace the faithfulness of Desmond Tutu and of other Christians who led South Africa peacefully out of the era of apartheid.

To acknowledge the beauty and appropriateness of the prophetic voice in the past is also to be aware that such language may be necessary in the present and certainly will be required in the future. It is the work of thoughtful Christians to pay attention and to discern when the use of biblical, prophetic language is needed.

IMMIGRATION AND THE PROPHETIC VOICE

When discussing the issue of immigration policy, for example, Christians with a variety of backgrounds who are attracted to any of Christendom's several traditional approaches to migration and to extending hospitality to sojourners can debate a variety of ideas and, in good faith, can either seek common ground or stake claim to a position on one of the extremes of the ideological spectrum.

However, when the discussion turns from a theoretical analysis of theology and policy to addressing the immediate needs of migrants who are refugees in danger of deportation back to the violence they have escaped, it can become necessary for Christians to look to something more foundational, to reach back before the development of Christian theology and, with thoughtfulness, to make use of the prophetic language and images that are canonized in Holy Writ. In no uncertain terms, the Bible demands both justice and kindness for immigrants[2] and sojourners and calls Christians to practice a faith with a commitment to the well-being of the poor and sore beset that is as dogged as it is thoughtful.

This can be problematic, of course. Prophetic language often is bombastic and aggressive. It calls out sin and names what is evil in the world. A prophetic vocabulary contains few words of compromise. It is, necessarily, self-righteous and self-confident. It is the language of Rosa Parks refusing to give up her seat on the bus, of Gandhi leading his followers to make salt at the sea in defiance of the English, of William Wilberforce working tirelessly for an end to the transatlantic slave trade. When used righteously, prophetic language will agitate and strengthen the resolve of those whose misdeeds make the rhetoric necessary; used inappropriately, prophetic words cause more harm than good. This is why prophetic discourse must be used sparingly and only after thoughtful consideration.

I would argue that thoughtfully prophetic language became necessary in 2014 when, in response to the most serious humanitarian crisis to hit the Western Hemisphere in decades, an unprecedented wave of migration brought refugees—many of them children—from Central America to the United States' southern border. The surge of immigrants overwhelmed an immigration and border protection service not prepared to care for large numbers of families or unaccompanied children, and it challenged a political system whose immigration policies have tended to address voluntary migrants looking for economic improvement rather than those displaced by violence.

The need for prophetic language to address the immigration crisis of 2014 became apparent to me when, through my work as a pastor, I became acquainted with a family who had escaped violence beyond anything I can imagine. Job,[3] the family's patriarch, is a clean-cut man without a lot of hard edges; he has the look of someone new to the work of his current employment—setting tile—which indeed he is. Before leaving San Pedro Sula in northwest Honduras, Job and his wife, Dolores, ran a pair of small businesses—he worked in retail, selling school supplies, and she had a restaurant—work that in the United States would be sufficient to qualify for membership in the Rotary Club. Their eldest child, Maria, who is nineteen, speaks fluent English. Before the family moved north, she worked at a call center providing offshore customer support for impatient American consumers.

Theirs was a good life in a troubled city. San Pedro Sula is one of the world's most dangerous cities,[4] but for Job, Dolores, Maria, and two other children, it was home. Job and Dolores made a decent living, Maria was working and was taking college courses on the side, and the two younger children were in school. All this changed, however, when a member of the Mara 18, a transnational drug gang with roots in Southern California, demanded a monthly "war tax" from Job and Dolores.

In San Pedro Sula—as in much of Honduras—gangs that started out in California prisons more or less operate as a shadow government. The gangs are violent and murderous, and part of what they do is extort the citizens living in the neighborhoods they control: those not willing to pay a "war tax" refuse at great risk to themselves and to their families.[5]

Job didn't want to pay the extortion, and he decided to seek protection from the Mara 18 by reporting the request to local police. The police responded by ratting Job out to the Mara 18. Within days, gang members came to the family home, beat Job to the edge of death, and raped Dolores and her thirteen-year-old daughter while their nine-year-old son looked on.

The family knew the Mara 18 would be back, and next time they would add murder to their list of crimes. The family decided to travel north, and within hours they were on their way to find safety in the San Francisco Bay Area, where Job's mother had been living for seven years and working as a housekeeper. The journey was not an easy one. Maria was just twenty days past giving birth (by C-section) to a son. The journey by bus across Guatemala and Mexico with a newborn infant was difficult, but when the family reached Matamoros, across the border from Brownsville, Texas, things got worse. Members of a Mexican drug cartel kidnapped the entire family the moment they stepped off the bus, demanding a $3,000 "fee" to smuggle the family into the United States. After a month, Job's mother in California was able to find the money and the coyotes (or human smugglers) ferried Dolores, Maria, the two younger children, and the baby into Texas, but they kept Job behind. Three weeks later they brought Job to the border and told him to climb the fence, which he did, and in the process he had a heart attack.

U.S. border patrol agents found Job and saved his life. After he spent a week at a hospital in Brownsville, the customs and immigration service released Job to join his family in California for the duration of the legal process that would determine whether or not they will receive asylum in the United States, a status only conferred upon those able to prove they are in danger in their countries of origin, which is difficult to do.

A HISTORICAL CONTEXT

It could be argued that the misfortunes of Job and his family are, while undeniably regrettable, not all that uncommon. People all over the world suffer, and no one is in favor of suffering. The Bible's prophetic language is meant to move the powerful, but everyone—including the powerful—already knows the gangs who make life hell in Central America are bad. So why waste our breath?

There are two reasons. First, no matter how bad things are in places like Honduras, many powerful Americans are opposed to immigration policies that would provide safety for the victims of Central American violence—this in direct contradiction to various biblical injunctions to care for immigrants,[6] and second, many of those responsible for the violence in Central America are powerful Americans who just might listen if we raise our voice in prophetic witness.

The violence that forced Job and his family to seek asylum in the United States did not happen in a vacuum. In fact, it comes as a direct result of American foreign policy in Central America. In the 1980s, when the region was playing host to several conflicts in which the Cold War grew hot, the United

States provided monetary and military support to governments (in El Salvador, Guatemala, and Honduras) and to a guerilla army (in Nicaragua), all of which had awful human rights records. (The governments and armies allied with the United States' geopolitical aims employed tactics such as "disappearance" by death squad, assassination, rape, and torture in an effort to stem the tide of political change.)

In Guatemala and El Salvador, civil wars pitted Marxist rebels against the armies of U.S.-backed dictatorships. In Nicaragua, following a 1979 coup and the establishment of a government with Marxist leanings, the United States trained and supported a counterrevolutionary force that fought a protracted and bloody war against the Nicaraguan regime. The war in Nicaragua spilled over into Honduras, whose right-wing government supported the U.S.-backed war against Nicaragua.

This mixture of warfare and human rights abuses created a refugee crisis as victims of war and torture left their homelands in search of safety. Refugees from Nicaragua had the option of fleeing south into Costa Rica (where the United Nations built camps to house them),[7] but those fleeing violence in Guatemala, El Salvador, and Honduras had one choice if they didn't want to cross through the killing fields of Nicaragua's bloody civil war: they had to go north. Sometimes they stopped in Belize and Mexico, but for many Central American refugees, heading toward the United States usually made the most sense. As a nation, it had the greatest freedom, least corruption, best public infrastructure, and the strongest economy.

Under international law—according to conventions signed by the United States—the United States has an obligation to welcome and to help resettle refugees within its borders[8]—a legal mandate that also happens to be a moral requirement for those whose faith is formed by Scripture. This proved problematic, however, because the United States supported the governments whose disregard for human and civil rights created the refugee crisis in the first place. To welcome refugees from Guatemala, El Salvador, and Honduras was to admit there was a crisis, which was to acknowledge wrongdoing in the region.

Politically, for the Ronald Reagan administration, that seemed an impossible thing to do.

So instead of granting refugee status to those fleeing warfare in Central America during the 1980s, American policy sent thousands of Guatemalans, Salvadorans, and Hondurans into the shadows of life as undocumented migrants. To be undocumented in the United States is to live a life of poverty, and in the rough and impoverished barrios of Los Angeles, migrants who might otherwise have met the requirements to be legally recognized as refugees encountered the culture of California's gang warfare. As the 1980s faded into the '90s and the immigration policies of the Clinton administration took effect, the United States began exporting the California gang culture to Central America in the form of deported undocumented persons who had been convicted of gang-related felonies and spent time in California's penal system.[9]

This was a disaster for Central America. In these nations struggling to recover from more than a decade of bloody wars, local law enforcement was not sufficiently equipped to deal with the arrival of gang members hardened by life on the mean streets of Los Angeles and by time spent in the violent cauldron that is California's criminal justice system. The power of the gangs grew, and twenty years later Central America is the world's most dangerous region, especially for women, and Job's family is hardly alone in its search for safety in the United States.

CHILDREN AT THE BORDER

In times of war and in places where crime runs rampant, often it is children who suffer most. This certainly is the case in the violence that grips Central America. Half of Job's family was under the age of eighteen (and Maria was only nineteen) when they crossed into the United States, but many of the children fleeing violence in Central America are not lucky enough to travel with the protection of an adult. Many children from

Central America travel and face the dangers of migration alone. In a study of the phenomenon of unaccompanied children crossing the U.S./Mexico border, the United Nations High Commissioner for Refugees found that

> beginning in October 2011, the U.S. Government recorded a dramatic rise—commonly referred to in the United States as "the surge"—in the number of unaccompanied and separated children arriving to the United States from . . . El Salvador, Guatemala and Honduras. The total number of apprehensions of unaccompanied and separated children from these countries by U.S. Customs and Border Protection (CBP) jumped from 4,059 in FY 2011 to 10,443 in FY 2012 and then more than doubled again, to 21,537, in FY 2013. At the same time, a tremendous number of children from Mexico have been arriving to the U.S. over a longer period of time, and although the gap is narrowing as of FY 2013, the number of children from Mexico has far outpaced the number of children from any one of the three Central American countries. For example, in FY 2011, the number of Mexican children apprehended was 13,000, rising to 15,709 in FY 2012 and reaching 18,754 in FY 2013. Unlike the unaccompanied and separated children arriving to the U.S. from other countries, including El Salvador, Guatemala and Honduras, most of these children were promptly returned to Mexico after no more than a day or two in the custody of the U.S. authorities, making it even more difficult to obtain a full picture of who these children were and why they were coming to the U.S.[10]

Many predicted the number of unaccompanied children crossing the U.S./Mexico border would reach ninety thousand by the end of the 2014 fiscal year. For Christians, the presence of children along the border adds a certain measure of urgency to our need to speak prophetically: joined to the Bible's call to care for immigrants are also biblical admonitions to care for orphans (Exod. 22:22 and Jas. 1:27, for example) and Jesus' stern warning—found in the twenty-fifth chapter of Matthew—that whatever we do to the "least of these" we to do him.

The children seek refuge in the United States (as well as in other countries, such as Costa Rica and Nicaragua) because El Salvador, Guatemala, and Honduras are among the poorest and most dangerous countries in the region. Nearly half of the children interviewed by the United Nations High Commissioner for Refugees "shared experiences of how they had been personally affected by the augmented violence in the region by organized armed criminal actors, including drug cartels and gangs or by State actors."[11]

It's not easy to accommodate ninety thousand children a year, which is exactly what the United States Customs and Border Protection has had to do, but even allowing for the logistical nightmare of the task, the Customs and Border Protection frequently has failed in its task to provide a safe and healthy environment for the unaccompanied immigrant children whom they have caught trying to cross the border. Not being organized or trained as a child welfare agency, the Customs and Border Protection has done what it knows how to do: it has thrown the children in jail.

Reports and photos from inside the detention centers show kids sleeping in chain-link cells. Other kids sleep wherever they can find a spot on cement floors, including on the bathroom floor. Said bathrooms being insufficient for the sheer number of children, the Customs and Border Protection agents provided port-a-potties for the kids and placed them inside the rooms where the kids were staying. Given the fact that port-a-potties are designed for outdoor use, the stench must have been horrendous.

Most of the children in photos from the detention centers are wearing shoes without laces, which is standard practice for the incarceration of adults. To take the laces from the shoes of children is to make it impossible for that child to play, and playing is part of the dignity and beauty of childhood. Some of the kids being detained in Arizona are less than a year old.

If the conditions endured by the undocumented immigrant children in detention centers wasn't sufficient to damage the well-being of the children residing there, anti-immigration activists in Southern California and Virginia thwarted efforts to move children in detention to smaller, presumably safer, cleaner, and more appropriate facilities in their communities. In Escondido, California, more than five hundred residents showed up at a planning commission meeting to oppose a proposal to house roughly a hundred children in a shuttered old-folks home. The protesters prevailed: the planning committee rejected the conversion of the unused facility by a vote of 7 to 0.[12] In nearby Murrieta, protesters waving American flags and chanting "USA! USA!" blocked three busloads of women and children bound for an immigration processing facility.[13] In Lawrenceville, Virginia, local residents balked at the suggestion that apprehended undocumented teens might be housed in the vacant campus of the recently shuttered St. Paul's University.[14]

How should a thoughtful Christian respond when children fleeing violence in Central America end up in overcrowded, unsanitary detention centers that are, for all intents and purposes, jails? How should a thoughtful Christian respond when self-proclaimed American "patriots" protest the resettlement of these children—many of whom, under international law, are legal refugees—with angry placards and words that speak of the children as criminal invaders? And how, for that matter, should a thoughtful Christian respond to the needs of people like Job and his family—people escaping violence created by U.S. policy but whose long-term safety in the United States is far from guaranteed?

RECLAIMING PROPHETIC LANGUAGE

It turns out that a lot of Americans are just fine with policies that prevent the migration of those fleeing violence in Central America. An Associated Press poll from the summer of 2014 found that most Americans wanted to see unaccompanied minor children from Central America deported without a hearing.[15] It's safe to say that even more Americans would rather see the United States deport Job and his family than grant them asylum and protection from the violence from which they fled. In a somewhat less scientifically reliable study, I found that my friends who used social media to post their support for the detention and deportation of migrant children tended to couch their support for the detention and deportation of children using the language of faith-based ethics. For these people, throwing innocent preschoolers in jail was a way of abiding by the rule of law, of protecting the innocent U.S. taxpayer, and of helping parents in Central America to take responsibility for their children. This was tough love.

Almost Christlike, really, if by Jesus, you mean Ayn Rand.

There are times when a thoughtful Christian must learn from what is old, must look to the Bible and to the great saints of the Church to find language with which to address injustice. In fact, sometimes a Christian has nothing to add if she or he does not speak with the language of faith, so that when a Christian suggests the United States is entirely correct to throw unaccompanied immigrant children in jail or when a secular talking head uses the language of "law and order" and "personal responsibility" to justify policies that might get Job's family sent back to their home in the world's most dangerous city, a Christian can argue about immigration policy, but so can anyone else. Sometimes if a Christian is going to speak in ways that are uniquely Christian, it is necessary, with the prophet Amos, to say, "Let justice roll down like waters, and righteousness like an ever-flowing stream!" (Amos 5:24). Or to quote the prophet Isaiah by saying, "This is the fast that I choose: to loose the bonds of injustice" (Isa. 58:6) or to speak the words of Jesus, who said, "Whoever welcomes this child in my name welcomes me" (Luke 9:48), and elsewhere said, "Just as you did it to one of the least of these who are members of my family, you did it to me" (Matt. 25:40).

This is archetypal, mythic, and prophetic language, and sometimes no other words suffice. After all, what can we say in response to hearing that our tax dollars are being used to imprison children? We could use legal language: we could point out that under federal law, no child under the age of eleven can be convicted of a crime, and we could point out, further, that under the United Nations' Convention on the Rights of the Child, a member state (which the United States is) cannot convict or detain children who are under the age at which it believes a child is capable of committing crimes. And when we are done talking about the law, we could talk about child psychology and we could talk about the children's various emotional, recreational, and educational needs. As people of faith we should be having those conversations, but unless we are lawyers or psychologists or social workers, we may not have much to offer in the conversation. However, as people of faith, what all of us can bring is ancient wisdom: ideas and words that in some cases date back to the Bronze Age and that have survived and remain holy because they speak deep truth as they call us to be better people living in a better world.

A thoughtful Christian has a working knowledge of the prophetic language of faith and is able, when need be, to use it appropriately. This can sound a little scary and perhaps even a little bit creepy—after all, how many of us have been condemned, degraded, and plagued with spiritual guilt because some Bible basher misused and misquoted Holy Writ in our general direction? That's why we must be thoughtful when we speak out in favor of justice and mercy and change using Scripture and the language of faith. But prophetic language is necessary. Think of what Martin Luther King Jr. would be without biblical language, or Mother Teresa or Oscar Romero or even Pete Seeger: What would they be without the ancient and powerful vocabulary of faith?

When used correctly, the language of faith gives our actions depth and beauty and power and meaning that secular language cannot impart. It's powerful and it should be used judiciously. For example, it would hardly be appropriate to quote the Bible or appeal to theological and spiritual traditions when arguing about who would make the best mayor, but when we are talking about critical moral issues, it's necessary. The safety of a family, the detention of children, the use of torture by the United States in its prosecution of the war on terror, capitalism that has become detached from its moral compass, unrestrained access to assault weapons, and the denial of rights for LGBT people: these situations require us to dust off the Bible and revisit transformative theological and spiritual traditions that have inspired justice in the past, for as thoughtful Christians we are part of a great tradition that is ancient but also very much alive.

The traditional language of our faith has power we can harness and use when we speak out against injustice. The language has been given to us by our spiritual foremothers and forefathers. It has been stewarded by Sunday school teachers and pastors and scholars, and it bears the weight of centuries of prayer and action. It has been refined by trial and error, and it is now ours to use as we seek to live out the gospel by making the world a better place for all God's children, especially, perhaps, the children of Job and the children of God who are imprisoned by the United States in Arizona for seeking safety. To speak with prophetic thoughtfulness on behalf of immigrants fleeing violence who have been harmed by American immigration laws or to speak prophetically against any act of injustice, hatred, or intolerance is to place oneself in the tradition of faithful Christians who have spoken out against slavery, resisted Nazism, and marched to end Jim Crow and apartheid. It is, in short, to stand where the Church, in its best days, always has stood.

5

Learning from What Is New

The Scripture does not change, but our power of entering into its meaning changes.

—Brooke Foss Westcott[1]

In 2006, my wife and I did something that was, in retrospect, a little bit crazy. We took a red-eye flight to Boston with three children under the age of five. Then we rented a minivan and drove several hours north so that we could attend (and, in my case, deliver the homily at) the wedding of our friends Chris and Julia in rural Maine. To a Californian (to *this* Californian anyway) two things about Maine—other than its stunning natural beauty—became immediately apparent. First, there is a singular lack of freeways in the Pine Tree State, and second, there seem to be two different states existing simultaneously in that beautiful land.

One expression of Maine is made up of darling hamlets that seem to have been designed by Martha Stewart using the L. L. Bean catalogue. The other Maine is one in which evidence of rural poverty is conspicuous. One Maine is marked by perfectly maintained summer cottages and general stores where tourists can buy maple syrup. In the other Maine rusted automobiles and logging equipment in disrepair decompose side by side in front of dilapidated mobile homes that look insufficient for a winter in northern California, much less in northern New

England. Frequently the two Maines—one comfortably blue-blooded and the other squalid and poor—are separated only by a few curves in the two-lane country roads that pass as state highways in that part of the world. In short, Maine, with its contrasting wealth and poverty, is a microcosm of America.

The wedding we attended was in the latter Maine, though Chris and Julia were not poor so much as young and just getting started. They had purchased an old puppy mill that once provided canines to second-rate New England pet stores, and they were in the process of remodeling the house and converting the barn into a studio space for painting, music, and dance. Julia was an excellent carpenter and a dancer. Chris was a musician and an artist. Both were passionate about setting down roots into the frequently frozen soil of rural Maine.

Prior to the ceremony itself, my family spent a few days enjoying Maine's natural beauty and attending typical pre-wedding festivities. On the morning of the ceremony, after we'd all put on our very best clothes, my then-four-year-old daughter made a startling realization: there was no groom. *Christine* and Julia were both brides, and while I wouldn't say explaining same-sex marriage to a four-year-old was easy, I found the task of explaining my participation in the ceremony to adult church-folk a much more delicate and difficult task.

When my family returned from Maine, with encouragement from the brides I wrote about the wedding on my blog and I spoke about it on a local public radio station. The responses were predictable: a couple of people with gay or lesbian siblings started coming to my church, but I also got a lot of really nasty e-mails and blog comments, at least one of which suggested that my participation in a same-sex wedding ceremony was contributing to the unraveling of Western civilization.

What my supporters and my detractors had in common was a desire to know how I could embrace same-sex marriage and still, with a straight face, call myself a Christian (and a clergyman at that). The people who came to my church as a result of my support for same-sex marriage (as well as those already there who were relieved to hear of their pastor's nontraditional views on the subject) wanted language with which to reconcile their love and support for the gay men and lesbians in their lives with the Christian faith that gave them meaning, peace, and joy. My detractors wanted to know what I was thinking so they could prove me wrong, which is perfectly reasonable. Theological debate is a time-honored tradition in the Christian community. Without debate the Church cannot grow or change or adapt. In short, without debate the Church dies.

But the Church hasn't died. The Christian faith remains a living tradition, and with each new generation, Christians must pay attention to what's happening in the world and then respond faithfully. A thoughtful Christian learns from what is new. This is a principle that explains why an otherwise traditionally minded Christian whose theology is rooted in the historical affirmations of the faith can celebrate the broader society's increasing embrace of marriage equality, but the principle is bigger than one issue. The idea that thoughtful Christians must learn from what is new explains a lot of the ways Christians have changed over the years.

A HISTORICAL EMBRACE OF CHANGE

For two thousand years, Christianity has changed when it has come in contact with new ideas, new information, new cultural norms, and new language. In fact, a careful reader of the New Testament will observe that adaptation is woven into the New Testament itself. This embrace of change is especially evident in the Bible's stories of the Christian Church changing and adapting to make room for non-Jewish believers. In the book of Acts, the debate around including Gentiles in the Christian Church begins as an argument between the apostle Peter and God, who, in anticipation of Peter's possible reticence to preach the gospel among non-Jews, shows Peter a vision of non-kosher animals and invites Peter to eat them. "Never!" cries the Rock Upon Whom the Church Was Built, "for nothing unclean has ever entered my mouth."

"Do not call unclean," replies the Creator of Heaven and Earth, "what I have made clean," and in response to the vision, Peter begins the work of evangelizing the pagan world.[2]

As the Church changed to include non-Jews, it also had to make adjustments in its requirement that all Christians must obey Jewish laws. Again, this transition is recorded in the book of Acts when the apostle Philip encounters a eunuch from Ethiopia on a road though the wilderness between Jerusalem and Gaza. The eunuch is reading a passage from the book of Isaiah,

> "Like a sheep he was led to the slaughter,
>   and like a lamb silent before its shearer,
> so he does not open his mouth.
> In his humiliation justice was denied him.
>   Who can describe his generation?
> For his life is taken away from the earth."[3]

The eunuch has some questions about the passage. Philip answers those questions, and the eunuch asks to be baptized. It sounds like a fairly straightforward case of one-on-one evangelism, but if the Ethiopian eunuch was reading the passage from Isaiah mentioned in the story, he almost certainly would also have read a passage found a few chapters later in the book of Isaiah that was not mentioned in Acts but that certainly was implied:

> Do not let the foreigner joined to the LORD say,
>   "The LORD will surely separate me from his people";
> and do not let the eunuch say,
>   "I am just a dry tree."
> For thus says the LORD:
> To the eunuchs who keep my sabbaths,
>   who choose the things that please me
>   and hold fast my covenant,
> I will give, in my house and within my walls,
>   a monument and a name
>   better than sons and daughters;
> I will give them an everlasting name
>   that shall not be cut off.[4]

This passage from Isaiah is responding to a set of laws found in the law of Moses that excludes eunuchs from the worshiping life of the temple. For example, Deuteronomy 23:1 says, "No one whose testicles are crushed or whose penis is cut off shall be admitted to the assembly of the LORD." Thus, the story of Philip and the Ethiopian eunuch becomes a fulfillment of Isaiah's prophecy of the day, in the fullness of time, when eunuchs would be included fully in the life of faith. This story gave the earliest Christians a theological framework upon which to build a Church in which non-Jews didn't have to follow Jewish laws.

The book of Acts is not the only place where these questions are addressed. The earliest surviving Christian writings are letters written by Saint Paul and preserved in the New Testament. Paul was active in the work of evangelizing non-Jews and was an early advocate of the idea that non-Jews shouldn't have to follow the Jewish law. Despite explicit directions from the Jerusalem Church leaders to the contrary,[5] Paul tells Christians living in the Greek city of Corinth that it's fine to eat meat sacrificed to idols (an absolute no-no according to the practices of the earliest Christians), provided they don't offend anyone when they do, and in one particularly terse bit of writing on the subject of whether or not male Gentile converts to Christianity should be circumcised, Paul expresses a desire that those who believe so strongly in the necessity of circumcision—and of abiding by Jewish law—should go all the way and castrate themselves.[6]

In the Gospels, which tell the story of Jesus' earthly ministry and which were written after the letters of Paul (and concurrently with the book of Acts), we see Jesus interacting with the same issues. In Matthew, the first people to recognize Jesus as messiah are foreign, pagan magi. In Mark, Jesus heals the child of a foreign woman after being convinced by her that her daughter is worthy of Jesus' ministrations even if she isn't Jewish. In Luke, the stories of Jesus' conception and birth (and the brief mention of his childhood) are told from the point of view of Jesus' mother, despite contemporary suggestions that women should be silent in church. In John, Jesus speaks with and receives a drink from a Samaritan woman, who is both female and ethnically impure.

All of this suggests change is written into the very DNA of Holy Writ. It would be possible, of course, for Christian readers of the Bible to assume that spiritual evolution was fine so long as everyone understands that the process of change ended as soon as the project of writing the Bible was complete, but among thoughtful Christians that hasn't happened. If the process of theological development ended with the death of the last apostle, then we'd still be arguing about circumcision, about welcoming eunuchs into our congregations, and about whether or not to eat meat sacrificed to idols.

But these are not the issues with which most of us[7] grapple. Most Christians I know are struggling with how faithfully to respond to issues like global climate change, the morality of war, economic inequality, education policy, abortion, racism, immigration, the role and scope of government, substance abuse, interfaith relationships, and (as mentioned above) human sexuality. Several of these issues—like climate change—were unheard of before the twentieth century, and while some of these issues were in some form present when prophets and apostles wrote the Bible, no one grappled with these issues as we grapple with them today. It's one thing, for example, to struggle with the morality of warfare when everyone is fighting with swords and spears; it's another thing altogether to talk about the ethics of violence in a post-Hiroshima world in which pilotless drones fire GPS-guided missiles at unsuspecting civilian populations.

WHEN CHANGE IS NEEDED

If, as Christians, we are going to practice a faith that, with thoughtfulness, evolves to address a changing world, then we must pay attention to what is happening in the realm of science and technology and then respond appropriately, even if it means we must reevaluate and adjust our understanding of what the Bible tells us so that when innovations come along, we have a place for those innovations in the Christian life. For example (as discussed in chap. 2), when the scientific community informs us that the burning of fossil fuels is releasing carbon dioxide into the atmosphere in ways that threaten all of life, we have to modify, reevaluate, or simply set aside any biblical interpretation that tells us God has given us the earth to use as we please.

But human learning and innovation is not limited to the realm of science, and just as our faith must make room for scientific innovation, so also our faith must make room for nonscientific innovations and understandings. We evolve politically, for example, and have shifted our thinking about the role of God in establishing the right of monarchs to rule over their subjects. For the first fifteen hundred years of Christian history, no one doubted the right of kings and queens to rule their kingdoms, nor was there any doubt that the relationship between monarchs and their realms was ordained by God Almighty. This conviction was rooted in Scripture: Romans 13:1 says, "Let every person be subject to the governing authorities; for there is no authority except from God, and those authorities that exist have been instituted by God," and for centuries it was a matter of settled theology. This is not to say that every Christian obeyed every royal decree, but those who, out of faithfulness to the gospel, disobeyed the laws and directives of their monarchs seldom doubted the right of a king or queen to his or her throne.

Then, in the middle of the sixteenth century, society began to change and the Church started to evolve. People like John Knox, the founder of the Presbyterian Church in Scotland, and to a lesser extent Knox's mentor, John Calvin, started to question the divine right of monarchs. Scotland has remained, at least nominally, a monarchy, but Knox's followers in North America played an important role in making sure that there would be no monarch in the United States, and no American Christian I know about is disappointed in this bit of societal and spiritual evolution. It turns out the Spirit shines new light on how we read the Bible, and a thoughtful Christian must pay attention.

Similarly, the Bible is clear in its support of slavery, but several hundred years ago, European and American Christians started listening to the voices of slaves, and, as a result, they had an innovative set of realizations: slaves are humans and should not be subjected to the indignity of slavery. Regardless of what the Bible says, it cannot be moral for one person to own another person. These ideas were evolutionary and rev-olutionary. It took a long time—in fact, the consensus that slavery is unjustifiable is less than a hundred and fifty years old, and even that estimate may be generous. For more than 90 percent of the life of the Christian faith, slavery was considered to be morally acceptable, but finally we have come to a point where no reasonable person appeals to the Bible to defend slav-ery. God's spirit has shined new light on the Scriptures, and thank God for that.

The same process is at work with human sexuality. The Bible tells us women are the sexual property of their fathers,[8] their husbands,[9] or their employers if they happen to be ser-vants.[10] The Bible also says that, in some circumstances, a raped woman must marry the man who attacked her.[11] But then, at some point, the keepers of Christian orthodoxy started listening to the voices of women, and through those women the Spirit's new light shone upon the Church's understanding of the Bible. This is not to say that every trace of misogyny has been expunged from the Christian faith—far from it—but we've moved in the right direction, and regardless of what the Bible says on the subject, I don't believe any of us want to go back. Nor should we.

This brings us back to a wedding in rural Maine, where two brides, after hearing me preach a homily, pledged their troth one to the other. There is no reason not to allow our under-standing of the Bible and our theology evolve as we listen to empirical data that tell us same-sex attraction is inborn and not a choice; nor is there any reason to ignore the voices of gay men and lesbians through whom the Spirit is shining new light. Our understanding of the Bible will necessarily change as will our theology, and lest this concept be misunderstood as some kind of new progressive rhetorical dance—a two-faced two-step in the double time of political correctness—let's remember that thoughtful Christians have been adjusting the way they read the Bible to accommodate new understandings since before there was a Bible to read, and in fact (as mentioned above), the Bible itself grew out of the experience of a changing Church.

An affirmation of marriage equality is a natural step in the evolution of Christianity in the twenty-first century, especially in light of the fact that same-sex marriage is gaining wider acceptance in the broader society. Indeed marriage equality is firmly established in most of the Western world, and there's no reason the Church and its membership should not also accept the changes to marriage already endorsed by secular society.

At the beginning of this chapter I wrote about economic inequality in rural Maine and, by extension, in the rest of the country. Most readers, no doubt, forgot about the descriptions of rural poverty once I got to the part about two women pledging their troth. Perhaps, in years to come, thoughtful Christians will care more about issues of economic inequality and of poverty than about love shared between two women. Surely that day is coming, for Christians continue to evolve and grow, and that is evidence of God's ongoing grace alive in the Church.

6

Embracing the Unknown

The Gospels, then, stand at the opening of a mystery in which
our lives are deeply, dangerously, and inescapably involved. . . .
It is a mystery that we are condemned but also are highly
privileged to live our way into, trusting properly that to our
little knowledge greater knowledge may be revealed. It is this
privilege that should make us wary of any attempt to reduce
faith to a rigmarole of judgments and explanations, or to any
sort of familiar talk about God. Reductive religion is just as
objectionable as reductive science, and for the same reason:
Reality is large, and our minds are small.

—Wendell Berry[1]

In the year 2000, on the seventh anniversary of my ordination,
I left San José for a pilgrimage that took me various places
in Scotland and England, including Oxford, which I visited
because I wanted to drink a beer in a pub called The Eagle
and Child. I realize that it may seem weird to travel halfway
around the world for a pint, but in my defense, when I was a
child, my fantasy life was formed more than anything else by
The Chronicles of Narnia by C. S. Lewis and by *The Hobbit* by
J. R. R. Tolkien. During college, my spiritual life was influ-
enced deeply by C. S. Lewis's popular theology—his allegorical
fiction and his nonfiction. These authors—Lewis and Tolkien
—were part of a group of writers who called themselves the
Inklings. They all were academics working at Oxford, and they
used to get together to drink and read their work to each other
at The Eagle and Child, and that is why I crossed a continent
and an ocean for a pint of bitters: I wanted to drink where
Lewis and Tolkien drank.

This was the last full day of my two-week stay in the United
Kingdom, so by the time I made it into The Eagle and Child,
I had been in several pubs. This one didn't look that different

from the others, except that on the walls were photos of my literary and theological heroes smoking, looking bleary-eyed, and surrounded by seemingly impossible numbers of empty pint glasses and overused ashtrays.

And so I had a pint of beer and a shepherd's pie, and I tried to soak up the vibe. When I was about halfway though my meal, there in the presence of some of my favorite saints, a young American couple walked in, and suddenly I wasn't the only spiritual pilgrim in the place.

I am the graduate of an evangelical college, and more often than not, we who graduated from places like Westmont or Hope or Houghton have a particular affectation. We can spot each other across crowded rooms, and this couple, like me, was from an evangelical college. I didn't actually talk to them, but they spoke to one another with midwestern accents, and so I'm guessing they were from Wheaton in Illinois or maybe from Calvin College in Michigan, but unlike me, they were not coming to Oxford for a beer. In fact, when they walked into the pub they got really funny looks on their faces. I could see the paradigm shifting in real time as they lived into the realization that their pilgrimage to connect spiritually with C. S. Lewis, that writer so loved and revered by conservative evangelicals everywhere, had led them directly into a saloon.

My fellow spiritual travelers ordered Diet Cokes and sat down in a corner. They looked with profound discomfort upon the photographic evidence that the author of *Mere Christianity* did not come to The Eagle and Child so that he could drink chamomile tea and that when he came to the pub, he brought his smokes with him, and with those little carcinogenic bad boys he filled to overflowing an untold number of ashtrays.

I have no idea which of C. S. Lewis's works inspired my fellow Americans to make their way to Oxford in search of his ghost. Christians who love the work of C. S. Lewis read all of his spiritual writing[2]—his popular theology, his memoirs, his allegorical fiction, and the fiction he wrote for children and adults—but I came to The Eagle and Child because I love C. S. Lewis's imagination, which is reflected in his fiction, allegorical fiction, and memoirs. It is this aspect of his work that continues to have a profound impact on my life, long after my affection for his theologically didactic popular nonfiction has waned. It is one thing to presume to be able to answer the questions raised by the fact that an all-loving and all-powerful God allows evil to exist (as Lewis does in his book *The Problem of Pain*), but it is another thing altogether to suggest, as Lewis also does, that whole universes might exist beyond the doors of a wardrobe and that the life of faith is informed not just by rational thought or by scientific discovery, but by being willing, like Peter, Susan, Edmund, and Lucy (the protagonists in *The Lion, the Witch and the Wardrobe*), to walk into the unknown through an ordinary piece of bedroom furniture.

Life is filled with mystery, and one of the reasons I believe Christianity still makes sense—despite everything—is that Christianity is rooted in the mystery that makes life wonderful and, sometimes, frustrating. After all, there is no belief more foundational to any religious tradition than the doctrines it uses to understand God, and when Christians talk about God, we do so using a mystery. We believe that God is three in one, one in three. Using traditional language, we would call God "Father, Son and Holy Spirit," or sometimes, "Creator, Redeemer, Sustainer," and—to complicate things further—when we talk about Jesus we say that he was human and God at the same time.

These are not rational ways to talk about God. This is not evidence-based theology. This is a surrender to mystery. The doctrine of the Trinity isn't even really found in the Bible. In the Bible there are a few places where all three members of the Trinity are mentioned, but the idea of God being one and three at the same time was developed later as early Christians reflected on the story of Jesus and as they experienced God alive in their communities and as they struggled to make their new experiences of the divine mesh with the Jewish beliefs out of which Christianity was born. The early Christians were committed to the idea of monotheism, but they had a hard time fitting all of the ways they experienced God into a single expression of God, so after nearly four hundred years of debate, and under duress from an imperial command that the Christians draw centuries of argument to a close and agree on an understanding of who God is, the doctrine of the Trinity became established Church doctrine.

Similarly, the Bible never actually says that Jesus was God and human at the same time. Sometimes it says Jesus was God, and sometimes it says he was human. This is confusing, of course, and over the years Christians had various ways of solving that confusion, of articulating how Jesus can have a dual identity as human and divine. Some considered Jesus to be fully human but endowed with an entirely God-like energy.[3] Still others felt that Jesus was God appearing as human but never actually being human. Then there were folks who considered Jesus to be both human and divine, but they also believed that because Jesus was human and divine, he must have been a creation of God and therefore not coeternal with God.

None of these explanations helped much. The early Christians really wanted Jesus to be both human and divine, but a divine human is a little bit like a round square. It doesn't work. However, at the same time the newly Christian-tolerant Roman emperors were forcing the Church to settle on the illogical Trinity, they also were requiring the Church to come to a conclusion about Jesus' identity. The Church went with the round square, deciding that Jesus is now, and forever has been, both human and divine.

Thus, in the fourth century of the Common Era the bishops of the Christian Church, meeting somewhat under duress, enshrined mystery as the cornerstone of the Christian faith, and upon that illogical theological foundation they built the Church. The unavoidable conclusion is this: a thoughtful Christian must necessarily be willing to learn from mystery. Just as the faith of a thoughtful Christian is molded by empirical information and scientific discovery, and just as a thoughtful Christian's theology and ethical decisions are shaped by Christian tradition, so also the spiritual life of a thoughtful Christian is informed by mystery. A thoughtful Christian must be willing to learn from what she does not know, indeed from what he cannot know. The thoughtful Christian must be willing to walk through the occasional wardrobe and into the mysteries that lie beyond.

This is counterintuitive, but keep in mind that there are many ways to learn, and much of what we know is not based in fact. When we are informed by mystery, we learn things like humility and patience and wonder and joy and delight, and those things inspire us and enable us to seek other kinds of knowledge. When we embrace mystery and when we learn from what we do not know, we are freed from any pressure that may be put upon us that we should have all of the answers, and when we are informed by unknowing, we must necessarily set aside any suggestion that those with whom we disagree should be scorned.

The doctrine of the Trinity roots us in mystery, as does the ancient Christian belief that Jesus was, at the same time, human and divine. I wish I could say that over the centuries Christians have interacted thoughtfully with mystery such that they have learned tolerance and open-mindedness and have embraced humility and have been at peace with everyone met, including and especially with other Christians. That has happened *sometimes*, but sadly, most Christians haven't been particularly comfortable with mystery. As a result, Jews, Muslims, pagans, dissident Christians, outspoken women, gay men, and lesbians have suffered. Millions have died because privileged and powerful Christians ignored the mysteries presented to them every time they went to church and heard a benediction in the name of the Triune God.

THE COST OF REJECTING MYSTERY

A person doesn't have to travel far to find evidence of the harm caused when Christians ignore the knowledge gained by learning from mystery—a visit to the local synagogue or mosque will suffice, but if a person is inclined to visit Zurich and knows just where to look along the west bank of the Limmat river, he or she can find a small piece of engraved granite—not much larger than an American license plate—that reads:

> Heir wurden mitten in der Limmat
> von einer Fisherplatform aus
> Felix Manz und fünf weitere Täufer
> en der Reformationszeit
> zwischen 1527 und 1532 ertränkt
> als letzter Täufer wurde in Zürich
> Hans Landis 1614 hingerichtet

Which, in English, means:

> Here, from a fishing platform
> in the middle of the Limmat,
> Felix Manz and five other Anabaptists
> from the Reformation period
> between 1527 and 1532 were drowned.
> The last Anabaptist executed in Zurich
> was Hans Landis in 1614.

I was in Zurich because I wanted to learn about the origins of the Anabaptist tradition, a movement that is important to me because my mother-in-law grew up in a denomination called the Brethren in Christ, which is part of the family of churches who trace their lineage back to the Anabaptists of Zurich. In fact my wife's grandmother's maiden name was Landis. She was descended—as are my wife and children—from the brother of the Hans Landis whose martyrdom is commemorated in granite along the banks of the Limmat.

Modern expressions of the Anabaptist tradition include such groups as the Amish, the Mennonites, and, as mentioned above, the Brethren in Christ, and to most modern people, Anabaptists come across as unlikely candidates for persecution. They have a tendency to dress old-school, and occasionally they drive horse-drawn buggies instead of cars, but that's more of a tourist attraction than a crime. They are pacifists, so there isn't much[4] chance they'll stage a coup. Often they won't participate in governments, which can be a problem because sometimes they won't pay taxes. But on the other hand, they also won't accept welfare or other forms of governmental assistance, and they won't organize politically or run for office.

Yet in their early years, the Anabaptists were persecuted severely. The Anabaptist movement started in the sixteenth century, at a time when political and ecclesiastical nonparticipation was not an option in most parts of Europe, and to the Anabaptists' offenses of nonconformity were added crimes of unacceptable theology. Most famously, Anabaptists rejected the idea of infant baptism, choosing instead to baptize adult believers. Also, they rejected Christianity's historic creeds, embracing the Bible as the sole theological authority in their congregations. Having rejected established churches, they worshiped as simply as possible in small, less formal settings. They were Protestants who took the theology and spirituality of the Reformation to radical conclusions.

In Europe during the sixteenth century it was hard for Anabaptists to find places where they could live peacefully and worship freely. In the Catholic parts of Europe, Anabaptists got in trouble for being Protestants, and in most of Protestant Europe, they suffered harassment for being the wrong kind of Protestant, but nowhere was their persecution more severe than in Zurich, the city where the movement began. As a result, my wife's forebears were forced to worship up in the hills, away from Zurich and far from the towns and villages whose spiritual and political lives were under Zurich's control.

The leader of the church in Zurich—and therefore the bane of the early Anabaptists—was a man named Huldrych Zwingli. Zwingli was a brilliant reformer. He was intelligent and well-educated, he was an excellent preacher, and (unlike many intelligent, well-educated, excellent preachers) he possessed a singular ability to organize and to motivate people. He also had a violent streak wide enough that often he was depicted holding a sword. The Anabaptists weren't the only recipients of Zwingli's wrath—he died in battle, fighting a coalition of Swiss cities with whom he had theological and political differences—but Anabaptists certainly felt the sharp end of

Zwingli's disapproval. As a result, most of Zurich's Anabaptists eventually left the city. From Zurich they spread out across the world. They found safety, for a time, in countries like the Netherlands and in cities like Strasbourg. Some sojourned for a time in the Ukraine, but ultimately the Anabaptists didn't find rest until they found their way to North America, where they established large communities in places like Pennsylvania, Ohio, Manitoba, Oregon, and California's San Joaquin Valley.

THE TÄUFERHÖHLE MYSTERIES

When reading history, it's probably better not to judge those who lived and died centuries ago according to modern values or to psychoanalyze historical figures using contemporary ideas about human development (something most of us aren't even qualified to do for the living). Yet, throwing caution to the wind, it's worth noting that Huldrych Zwingli was a man committed to learning. His dedication to the Reformation cause was rooted in humanism. He was a student of Erasmus, and he had a scholarly knowledge of biblical Greek and Hebrew. He was well-versed in the theological traditions that preceded him, and like most Reformers, he embraced science and other modes of gathering and analyzing empirical information. All of that knowledge informed Zwingli's theology and his ideas about how a Reformed Church should be organized. What Zwingli seems to have lacked was an appreciation for mystery and for the ability of the unknown to form and to inform faith. This inability to embrace mystery deprived Zwingli of the humility that comes as a result of contemplating the unknown. Thus, armed with certitude and self-assurance, the leader of Zurich's reformation undertook the work of slaughtering Anabaptists.

Zwingli's lack of appreciation for mystery is, perhaps, most evident in his sacramental theology. Whereas the Roman Catholic Church believed the body and blood of Christ is actually present at the Eucharist—so much so that the elements are transformed (a doctrine entirely dependent upon imagination and the embrace of what is unknown and unprovable)—and whereas Luther and his followers believed the body and blood of Christ to be substantially—if not physically—present at the Lord's Supper, for Zwingli the sacrament was a memorial feast entirely devoid of mystery. If, for Catholics and Lutherans, the key words of institution were "this is my body," for Zwinglians, the important statement at Communion was "do this in remembrance of me."

It's hard to know for sure if early Anabaptists were any more attracted to mystery than were their Zwinglian persecutors. If the places in which we worship teach us anything, if they convey meaning, for example, by having stained glass windows or not or by having a pulpit or an open platform and a big video screen worth more than a small German automobile, then at least some of the early Anabaptists learned about mystery by worshiping in a cave, in the hills southeast of Zurich far away from the cities and towns, where seditious singing and expository preaching would not be overheard by zealous church leaders in Zurich.

While traveling in Switzerland I visited the above-mentioned cave that served as an Anabaptist Church. It was January, and it was an adventure I took with one of my brothers, who joined me on the trip. Even with the aid of such modern conveniences as photocopied maps, hints for finding the place downloaded from the internet, sturdy shoes designed to compensate for pronating feet, and a warm jacket from L. L. Bean, it was hardly the kind of journey most Americans would be willing to undertake in order to worship with like-minded Christians. The casual pilgrim could drive most of the way from Zurich to the Anabaptist cave (or *Täuferhöhle*, as they say in German), but looking for adventure (and being too cheap to rent a car), we took a commuter train from Zurich to the town of Wetzikon and then a bus into the hills, to a smaller town called Bäretswil. From there we continued farther into the hills on foot, to the tiny hamlet of Wappenswil. There we turned onto an icy logging road that led higher and deeper into the hills, to a place called Holenstein, which is too small even to be called a village. In Holenstein the roads (such as they were) ended, and we continued by trail through ankle-deep snow, up a steep meadow, and then into the woods along the edge of a deep ravine.

It was a magical place—quiet, save for the water of a stream and the occasional bird. As we walked through the snowy woods, we half expected to find a streetlamp and, perhaps, a faun bearing gifts, for the place resembled Narnia as Lucy discovered it beyond the wardrobe's doors in *The Lion, the Witch and the Wardrobe*.

Finally (and, alas, without the aid of talking creatures) we found the Anabaptists' cave. Its mouth looked something like a giant eye at the end of a gulley, with a waterfall cascading down directly over the center of the cave's opening. Inside, a few benches were arranged like pews, and there was a memorial plaque to remind us that, after a long journey, we had come to a house of worship.

The cave isn't particularly big. At its highest point, twelve feet separate the ceiling from the floor. Altogether, the cave wouldn't provide space for a large congregation—a gathering of more than fifty people would require a lot of stooping and squatting at the back of the cave.

If the great cathedrals of Europe communicate something of the power and majesty of God, if a small clapboard chapel in rural America communicates the enduring faithfulness of God, and if a storefront church in the inner city communicates something of God's promises for a more hopeful and prosperous tomorrow, then the *Täuferhöhle*, by taking a congregation into the earth, speaks of God's mystery. There really is no way to know for sure if the Anabaptists worshiping in the cave were inspired by the mystery communicated by their sanctuary, but it's hard to imagine they would come away unaffected.

Like Zwingli and his followers, the Anabaptists weren't interested in worshiping in fancy surroundings, and their sacramental theology—especially as it related to baptism—was, if anything, even less reliant upon mystery than was Zwingli's. Yet when Anabaptists remember those among their number who died as martyrs during the time Zwingli and others forced the Anabaptists to worship in caves, they tell stories infused with mystery.

For example, Anabaptists often tell the story of Dirk Willems, a Dutch Anabaptist arrested and imprisoned for his faith who escaped from his jail by fashioning a rope out of rags and rappelling down over the walls of the castle that held him captive. Willems was a little overconfident in his sneakiness, however. A guard saw him coming over the wall and pursued Willems as he ran out over the frozen moat that surrounded the prison. Willems, having lost weight while in prison because the rations were meager, made it across the moat safely, but the guard, whose diet was a bit more hearty, broke through the ice and would have drowned except that Willems heard his cries for help and went back to save his erstwhile pursuer. Once pulled from danger, the saved man promptly arrested Willems; local authorities condemned Willems and burned him at the stake.

Why did Willems turn back? Certainly not because he was inspired by rational thought. It's much more likely that Willems was inspired by Jesus' call to love one's enemy, to forgive one's persecutors, and to turn the other cheek when struck. These actions are not based in fact; rather they trust in the *koan*-like mystery of the Beatitudes, which promise,

> Blessed are those who are persecuted for righteousness' sake, for theirs is the kingdom of heaven. Blessed are you when people revile you and persecute you and utter all kinds of evil against you falsely on my account. Rejoice and be glad, for your reward is great in heaven, for in the same way they persecuted the prophets who were before you.[5]

It is the kind of mystery more at home in a cave in the woods than in a great cathedral.

CAVES OF PERSECUTION TODAY

Whether or not the early Anabaptists were affected by the mystery of the cave that served as their church in the early and formative years of the tradition, my own encounter with the mystery as I walked though the wardrobe that took me out of my comfortable existence and into the Narnia of a snowy wood in the foothills of the Swiss Alps provided me with fresh insight into how American Christians interact with religious traditions they fear by claiming to be oppressed all the while working overtime to deny others—the First Amendment notwithstanding—the privileges they enjoy for themselves.

I came to the cave during winter because I wanted to experience the place at a time when visiting the Anabaptists' sanctuary would be least like going to my own church, a heated building in a temperate clime a mere three miles from my house. I got my wish, more or less. The day was cold. The woods were filled with snow, and icicles hanging from the top of the cave's opening looked like giant eyelashes, but still, it was warm enough that the creek was not frozen, and the wind did not howl, and the sky was blue.

It could have been a lot worse, yet to me the cave still felt cold and damp. A well-used fire pit near the mouth of the cave suggested the possibility of warmth, and the view looking out of the cave and into the wintery woods was charming and serene, but I couldn't help wondering if I would come all this way for worship. I'd make the journey for summer camp without complaint, but could I visit such a cave every Sunday, or even once a month, to engage in corporate worship, an activity that could get me banished from my home or even killed? That's an answer that gets a little bit trickier.

What I *can* say is that I'm glad I live in a place where Christians do not treat one another as poorly as they treated one another five hundred years ago in Europe. This is a new development. In fact, Christians have been oppressing and punishing and killing one another over small details of theology and practice for much of our two thousand years of existence.

And when it comes to people of other faiths—Jews, say, or Muslims—our track record is even worse: witness two thousand years of pogroms, crusades, inquisitions, and ongoing injustice born of fear, nurtured by ignorance, and fed by arrogance. In modern America, Muslims are the targets of Christian misbehavior, especially when Muslims try to build houses of worship. The Christian response to the erection of mosques makes me wonder if, given their preferences, American Christians would force their Muslim neighbors to worship secretly in frozen caves, deep in forests and far from cities.

Every once in a while I hear American Protestants complain that they are oppressed. Usually this has something to do with experiences in the public schools: a child forced to learn evolutionary biology or kept from singing "Silent Night" at a Christmas—or rather, "Winter Holiday"—program or not being allowed to say a prayer during a commencement ceremony or before a football game. American Protestants have teams of lawyers and lobbyists who are willing, at a moment's notice, to fight against such abuses by the secular powers that be.

I thought about the American Protestant sense of persecution as I sat shivering in the Anabaptist cave under a waterfall a the top of a gulley in the hills southeast of Zurich. It struck me that until we are forced to worship in caves, we should knock off talking about how persecuted we are, especially at a time when all across America, Christians are joining forces with social conservatives to prevent Muslims from building mosques in places that are convenient for worship. If I had my way, American Christians would only talk about persecution as a way of making sure we who hold places of cultural privilege never use the political and societal power we have to treat people of any other religious persuasion in such a way that they begin to feel the need to worship in caves.

MYSTERY DISARMS

It is far better to support Muslims who want to build mosques or Jews who feel disinclined to celebrate Christmas in public schools than to be the kind of person who would deny religious freedom to others, all the while claiming to be oppressed and sore beset. There is a self-indulgence inherent to those who, because they are unwilling to embrace mystery, assume their faith uniquely is victimized by the intolerant. Sometimes that self-indulgence leads to tragedy.

Such was the case on January 7, 2015, when armed gunmen stormed the offices of satirical newspaper *Charlie Hebdo* in Paris, killing a dozen people, including two policemen and four cartoonists who had drawn images of the Prophet Muhammad that many Muslims found offensive.[6] The gunmen made an escape, and their murderous rampage continued. The manhunt lasted three days and ended with sieges at a printshop where the gunmen had taken hostages and at a kosher supermarket where a third gunman apparently connected to the *Charlie Hebdo* attacks killed four hostages.[7]

In response to the *Charlie Hebdo* attacks there was an uptick in violence against Muslims in France. Several mosques came under attack[8] as right-wing politicians and talking heads across Europe doubled down on their anti-Muslim rhetoric.[9]

The murderous attacks in Paris and the Islamophobic reprisals that followed were a poignant reminder that we live in a world where too few people have walked through a wardrobe to try and recognize all that they cannot understand. Of this I am confident: no one who has embraced mystery, who faces all that is unknowable in the universe and beyond, who is unafraid to say "I could be wrong" will ever presume to engage in violence in the name of God or of any other ideology. If the truth of God makes us wise, the love of God makes us benevolent, and the grace of God frees us from sin, then surely the mystery of God must keep us sane.

7

Loving Knowledge

What is that which gleams through me and strikes my heart without injury, making me shudder and burn? I shudder inasmuch as I am unlike it, and I burn inasmuch as I am like it. It is Wisdom itself that shines through me, clearing my cloudiness, which so readily overwhelms me.

—St. Augustine of Hippo[1]

On September 6, 2013, a disturbing bit of email washed up over the digital transom of my in-box. With the words "Will your beheading interrupt, or enhance, sweeps week?" in the subject line, the sender—with whom I had neither prior nor subsequent acquaintance—posed the following challenge:

How about asking your Muslim masters to explain to your congregation how the butchering of Christians by their child molesting, animal torturing, sub human, cretinous brothers is a peaceful, positive message of love and tolerance for Christians? I'm sure we are just not getting the message, or just not appreciating their ethnic cleansing efforts enough. Oh, and speaking of efforts, be sure and let a real journalist, not one of the mindless, soulless minions currently contaminating the airwaves, know when your master will have his Islamic tools reward you for your efforts on his behalf, I'm sure your beheading will be the top story of the day.

For the next few hours, my smartphone doinked the arrival of several bits of similar correspondence until eventually I Googled myself in an effort to discern what, in the name of

Santiago Matamoros, was going on. My search rendered a post on a blog called *Bare Naked Islam* (tagline: "it's not Islamophobia if they really are trying to kill you") that began with the following words:

> Aren't there enough Islamofascists in America trying to sell their crap sandwich that Islam is a religion of peace? Now there's a *dhimmi* Presbyterian pastor pushing his crap book to churches about why our justified fear and loathing of Islam is without merit. How about sending him to Syria? I would love to post a video of this moron having his head cut off by al-Qaeda over there.[2]

The blog ended by providing my email address to those consumers of fear and hatred who migrate to such websites (as of this writing *Bare Naked Islam* boasted nearly sixty million individual hits).

One of the marks of thoughtful Christianity is curiosity born of a love for learning. Curiosity is something I've tried to foster as a spiritual discipline in my own life, and it was this attempt at faithful curiosity that ultimately got me in trouble with violent anti-Muslim activists who dreamed of my demise somewhere in the sands of the Syrian desert.

In the aftermath of the terror attacks of September 11, 2001, I became curious about the uptick in Islamophobia in American culture, and in an attempt to foster curiosity as a spiritual discipline, I started asking if there was any truth to the anti-Muslim rhetoric so dominant in public discourse. Ultimately, my curiosity led me to write a book that attempts, among other things (and with varying degrees of success, no doubt), to address the fear with which many American Christians regard Islam. I did this using information that is both reliable and useful but that might not be found on, say, Fox News. For example, while many American Christians fear a significant number of Muslims are terrorists, in my book I used a fairly basic (by which I mean even a pastor can do it) analysis of widely available empirical data to suggest the chances a randomly selected Muslim—taken from the world's 1.5 billion followers of Islam—will be a member of a known terrorist group are similar to the chances that five cards dealt off the top of a well-shuffled deck of cards will render a straight flush.

Many American Christians also fear Islam because they have heard from purveyors of fear that women living under Sharia in predominantly Muslim countries are unusually oppressed and sore beset. While it is true that life, for women, is hard in much of the Muslim world, as I researched my book I found empirical data that suggest this probably has more to do with poverty than it has to do with religion. Many predominantly Muslim countries are poor, and economics, not faith, is the most significant predictor of a woman's well-being. It's also true, based upon objectively measured rates of femicide (the crime of killing a woman because she is a woman) that for women, the world's most dangerous region is Central America, where almost everyone is some kind of Christian. Empirical data also inform us that infant mortality (a good measure of women's access to health care) is lower in several Muslim nations than it is in the United States. And while it is true that women in Saudi Arabia still may not drive or vote, it also is true that in September of 2014 a female pilot from the United Arab Emirates commanded a squadron of F-16s in an attack on ISIS positions in Syria[3] and that Pakistan—by population the world's second-largest Muslim nation—had a female head of state before the last women in historically Christian Switzerland had the right to vote in local elections.[4]

WHY CURIOSITY MATTERS

Most American Christians don't know a whole lot about Islam. Of course, Islam is not the only subject about which Americans—including Christians—lack knowledge. In fact, most American Christians don't even know basic information about Christianity (see the introduction to this book), yet every day the sun still rises and each year baseball follows spring training.

The difference is that while we fill the void left by our igno-rance of Christianity with a knowledge of what it means to keep up with the Kardashians or with other secular pursuits, when it comes to Islam, we fill the emptiness of our infor-mation storehouses with fear. Driven by that fear, we become dangerous, and as a result, innocent people suffer if they hap-pen to be (or are suspected of being) Muslim.

This is not merely the speculation of a politically correct, progressive preacher. The Council on American-Islamic Rela-tions (or CAIR), America's largest Muslim civil liberties orga-nization (think Anti-Defamation League or NAACP, only Muslim), documented a steady rise in reported civil rights abuses against Muslims between 1996, when fewer than a hun-dred reports of civil rights abuses were filed, and 2008 (the last year CAIR released numbers), when CAIR fielded more than 2,700 complaints. CAIR is not alone in reporting an uptick in abuses against Muslims. In 2009, the federal govern-ment's Equal Employment Opportunity Commission received 803 reports of workplace discrimination against Muslims—a 20 percent increase over the previous year. The high rate of abuse suffered by American Muslims also has been noted by a wide range of civil and human rights organizations, includ-ing Amnesty International, the Anti-Defamation League, the American Civil Liberties Union, the Southern Poverty Law Center, and Human Rights Watch.

In 2011, the Pew Center for People and the Press reported that 28 percent of Muslims report being looked at with suspi-cion, 22 percent say they have been called offensive names, 21 percent have been singled out by airport security, and 13 per-cent have been singled out for scrutiny by various law enforce-ment agencies. As animosity toward Islam has risen in the United States, so have reported incidents of hate crimes target-ing people of Middle Eastern descent and South Asians (espe-cially Sikhs), and others who are mistaken for Muslims.[5] When we leave unchecked the assumption that Islam is a religion of inherent violence and repression and assume every Muslim to be a potential enemy of freedom and decency, to ignore the witness of truth is to condemn Muslims to outsider status in our communities and in society at large.

It is an uncomfortable fact that the above-documented rise in civil rights abuses propagated against American Muslims correlates to a rise in fear of and prejudice toward Muslims in the wider American population. In 2003, 34 percent of Americans believed that Islam is a religion that encourages violence. Five years later that number had risen to 48 percent. By 2010, half of Americans harbored negative opinions about Islam.[6] A 2006 *USA Today*/Gallup Poll found that fewer than half of Americans believe U.S. Muslims are loyal to the United States and that nearly a quarter of Americans would not want a Muslim neighbor. Almost a third of Americans would be nervous if they noticed a Muslim man flying with them on an airplane, and 18 percent would feel similarly nervous if the Muslim were a woman. Forty percent of Americans believe Muslims *should* be subjected to increased security in public places.[7]

Americans, it turns out, aren't particularly well-informed. We tend to fear people about whom we know very little, and we allow that fear to manifest itself in a deprivation of dignity and civil rights. The antidote to this cycle of fear and oppression is wisdom born of a love of knowledge that starts with basic curiosity. A thoughtful Christian is curious enough to ask questions and, from there, to gather reliable information that renders knowledge, which matures into wisdom and makes us better people who form a more just, equitable society.

To say that Americans are uninformed is not to say that we don't consume information. Rather, it is to lament the fact that too much of what we consume is not equal to the task of making us smarter. An important step in the process of sating curiosity in a way that builds knowledge and eventually leads to wisdom is discerning which sources of knowledge are worth one's time. There are, after all, any number of purveyors of unreliable information—especially online and in the overly politicized space that is cable television. There is, alas, no universal formula that can be used magically to thresh the wheat of useful and reliable information from the chaff of malarkey that far too often passes for intelligent discourse, but there are some good starting points.

First (and this is fairly basic), if a magazine, website, book, radio program, or TV show seems focused primarily on encouraging the marginalization or hatred of a particular group of people, it's probably not worth the time. Similarly, if a news or information outlet seems overly political, it's a good idea to hear what is said—or read what is written—with the source's political bias in mind. If some bit of information seems a little less than reliable, it's worth taking the time to do an internet search to verify facts. In the end, the best way to find good sources for information is to spend a lot of time interacting with as much information as possible from a variety of sources. Eventually, that which is useful and valuable will become apparent.

There is no guarantee that a sudden awakening of American curiosity would wipe every manifestation of prejudice and mistreatment of Muslims from our society's record of sins: sometimes the curious consume bad information, and not everyone will make the progression from being curious to being wise, but it's impossible to believe more curiosity and a more robust commitment to learning wouldn't lead to at least a little more societal wisdom. At the very least, an intentional effort on the part of thoughtful Christians to discover and disseminate reliable information about Islam would realign us with the tradition of learning that has marked the best moments of the Christian Church throughout history and that helped to shape the Reformed branch of Protestantism at its inception.

MARGUERITE DE NAVARRE

Living as we do, in an era when feminist contributions to historical analysis have begun to seep past the gaskets that seal academia off from the broader society, it may seem superfluous to point out that the stories of women who have shaped Western history usually are overlooked, but unfortunately, most of us still need to be reminded that far too many historical accounts ignore the women who shaped the world we inhabit. Among the great historical figures largely forgotten for lacking a Y chromosome is Marguerite of Navarre, without whom the Calvinist branch of Protestantism might not have sprouted forth from the trunk of the Christian tree and a woman who, as much any other individual I know about, embodied one of thoughtful Christianity's central virtues: she loved knowledge. She was curious, she collected information, and she became wise.

Marguerite d'Angoulême, duchesse d'Alençon, reine de Navarre (her full title, in French) was born in 1492 to Charles d'Angoulême and Louise of Savoy in the city of Angoulême in western France. Her father was heir to the throne of France and her mother—from whom she seems to have inherited her intelligence—possessed one of the brightest minds in Europe. Marguerite married twice—once to Charles IV, duke of Alençon, and later, after Charles' death, to Henry II, king of Navarre, a small kingdom along what today is the French-Spanish border.

Though she was, by marriage, both a duchess and a queen, she is most famous (insofar as anyone remembers her) for being the sister of Francis I, the king of France. As the sister of the king, Marguerite wielded significant political clout. On one occasion she used this power to negotiate the release of her brother from the custody of the Holy Roman Empire after the French army suffered a humiliating defeat at the battle of Pavia; she also held a position of considerable social and cultural influence that she used to help change the course of Western history.

Marguerite had an unquenchable thirst for knowledge, and during her life she gathered unto herself a remarkable collection of brilliant people. Leonardo da Vinci—who, at the time, was redesigning and remodeling one of the royal French chateaux—died while living in Marguerite's home. François Rabelais, a clergyman famous for writing books that were both thought-provoking and scandalously ribald, enjoyed her friendship (which probably protected him from excommunication), and while he was a student at the Sorbonne in Paris, the future reformer John Calvin was a regular guest in Marguerite's salon.

HUMANISM

While it may seem remarkable that Marguerite should enjoy the company and friendship of both Rabelais and Calvin, it's worth noting that Marguerite—like the bawdy priest and the notoriously prudish reformer—was deeply affected by humanism, the Renaissance-era intellectual movement that sought to understand human concerns and that celebrated human accomplishments rather than focusing exclusively upon theological ideas and spiritual pursuits, which had been the primary work of medieval learning.

During the Renaissance, Christian humanists rediscovered the work of Latin and Greek poets and philosophers; they also rediscovered the beauty and power of biblical Greek and Hebrew. The rediscovery of classical philosophy led humanists to reconsider the importance of math, science, and secular philosophy. The renewed interest in Greek and Hebrew enabled humanist scholars to read the Bible in the languages of its authors.

All this learning—secular, sacred, linguistic, philosophical, and scientific—inspired many humanists to reevaluate the role religion should play in society and in individual human lives: not as a set of spiritually inclined ideas and propositions sealed off from other modes of learning, but as a fully integrated academic discipline that interacts with the sciences and the humanities.[8]

Among the leaders of the humanist movement in France were Jacques Lefèvre d'Étaples, who, though he remained Catholic, translated the New Testament into French and was a proponent of the kind of personal connection to the Divine (as opposed to a spirituality mediated by the Church) that later became a mark of Protestant Christianity. Lefèvre's students included William Farel, who later would precede and eventually work alongside John Calvin in the reformation of French-speaking Switzerland, and Guillaume Briçonnet, bishop of Meaux, whose diocesan reforms—including the public reading of the Bible in French—caused many within the Church to suspect he had become a Lutheran.[9]

Marguerite welcomed Lefèvre and his followers into her circle of intellectual friends, eventually making Briçonnet her spiritual advisor. This was fortuitous for Marguerite's proto-Protestant friends. When the fickle winds of French religious politics changed, Marguerite used her influence to protect the men whose inclinations she shared. When John Calvin first felt compelled to flee Paris after his Protestant leanings landed him in hot water, he went to Angoulême, the queen of Navarre's hometown, where he began work on the book that, over the course of twenty years, would evolve into Calvin's magnum opus, the *Institutes of the Christian Religion*.[10]

After a few months it became apparent that Calvin was not safe, not even in Marguerite's hometown. After brief visits to Paris and to his childhood home, Calvin left France. His plan was to join like-minded reformers in the city of Strasbourg, but as he made his way to the Alsace, he stopped to spend the night in Geneva. There he met the above-mentioned friend of Marguerite, humanist theologian and reformer William Farel, under whose ministry the Genevans were working to establish Protestantism in the city. Farel convinced Calvin that the church in Geneva needed his intelligence, his commitment to humanist Protestant theology, and probably most of all, his organizational acumen. Under duress—thanks to Farel's considerable powers of persuasion—Calvin stayed, and with the exception of a short exile in Strasbourg (where he got married, wrote poetry, and was, perhaps for the only time in his life, happy), he lived in Geneva for the rest of his life.

Though Marguerite remained a Catholic, the Calvinist branch of the Reformation, which was born in her living room, blossomed in Geneva under her patronage and protection. Calvin reformed the Genevan church with Marguerite's encouragement, and when the city fathers sent Calvin into the above-mentioned happy exile, the queen interceded on the preacher's behalf. Geneva relented, and, reluctantly, Calvin returned.

Eventually Calvin and Marguerite had a falling-out—she wasn't reformed enough for him in later years—but the work accomplished in Geneva, in part at her behest, changed the world by inspiring the reformation in Scotland; the Netherlands; much of England, Germany, and Hungary; and parts of France and Italy as well. Calvin's followers in Scotland—moved indirectly by Marguerite—started schools in every neighborhood of every Scottish city and in every Scottish town and village. As a result, Scotland became the most literate nation in the world, Scottish Presbyterians in North America founded more than a hundred colleges and universities, and the humanist spirit of Marguerite d'Angoulême, duchesse d'Alençon, reine de Navarre lives on. Or at least it's supposed to.

THE IDEAL AND THE REAL

The idea that Christians should learn—should be curious, gather information, gain knowledge, and attain wisdom—may seem entirely self-evident and obvious, especially for those Christians who read the Bible, paying serious and sober attention to its words and meaning. For example, the eighth chapter of the book of Proverbs speaks of wisdom—the goal of our curiosity and learning—as being the first thing God created and the means by which everything else is created. Proverbs presents wisdom as the highest goal to which a human can aspire, and here it's important to distinguish between knowledge and wisdom. Knowledge is the accumulation of information; wisdom is an ability to use information in a positive way. Knowledge makes us smart; wisdom makes us good. In the book of Proverbs, the path to wisdom—curiosity, the gathering of information, the attainment of knowledge, and finally achieving wisdom—is all laid out and recommended in fairly straightforward poetry.

In the New Testament, the Gospel according to John begins with the words "in the beginning was the Word," which is another way of saying, "in the beginning was Wisdom; and the Wisdom was with God, and the Wisdom *was* God." The ancient Hebrew writer of Proverbs imagined Wisdom as a child, a girl playing on the workbench of God, inspiring God and working with God to create the world.[11] The Greco-Roman Jewish Christian writer of John's Gospel took it a step further by saying that Wisdom, that first born child of God through whom everything was made, wasn't just like God but *was* God.[12]

Yet in the almost two thousand years since the Gospel of John gave Wisdom a promotion, upgrading her from God's first creation to God's self, the Christian Church has had a mixed record when it comes to learning and being wise. In our early years we moved, with disturbing speed and ease, from being a Jewish sect to being a fountainhead of anti-Semitic venom. We argued with one another and excommunicated one another over theological trivialities. In the Middle Ages, we engaged in bloody wars and called them holy; we invented cruel methods of torture and used them in inquisitions against Jews, Muslims, Cathars, and women suspected of witchcraft. Later, we devised religious justifications for the genocide of the pre-Columbian population of the Americas. As time marched on, we invented apartheid, rejected science, fought bloody wars in every corner of the globe, and sat, mesmerized by our televisions, as telegenic televangelists scammed us.

But not always. From time to time we've shown ourselves capable of the kind of learning that leads to wisdom. We founded some of the world's most important universities, and we preserved and copied manuscripts before we invented movable type, an innovation that made learning available to a much wider swath of humanity. We sculpted and painted and made music and wrote great poems and novels and plays. We founded hospitals and discovered new and good ways to heal people.

Learning is in our spiritual DNA, and sometimes we have used that learning to do good. Though we certainly made use of the peculiar institution, Christians didn't invent slavery, but by using the wisdom we gained through learning, we played an important role in ending it. We were not the first religious community to hold members of other faiths in low esteem, but some Christians have possessed wisdom sufficient to inspire interfaith goodwill that has brought healing and hope to places of ancient animosity. Christians have perpetuated the human vices of racism, misogyny, homophobia, and classism, but some of us also have used the wisdom natural to our tradition to work toward building a society of equality, acceptance, and universal dignity.

ISLAMOPHOBIA, REVISITED

It would be nice to end the chapter here, with the observation that Christians, though far from perfect, have embraced learning and wisdom and have marched out of a gloomy past, building communities and societies where the waters of deep justice, born of clear-thinking reason, nurture the roots of the commonweal. If that were the case, there would be no need for a reminder of the importance of learning, of being curious, of discovering new information, attaining knowledge, and becoming wise. Truly I wish this chapter didn't need to be written, but I think despite the witness of our history, we followers of Jesus still are not known by our overabundance of wisdom or our commitment to learning.

The urgent need to reclaim the legacy of Marguerite of Navarre leads us back to where this chapter began, to the fear in which many American Christians hold Muslims and Islam, for it is a fear born of ignorance and a dire lack of the simplest and most basic curiosity. If a talking head on cable news presumes all Muslims to be guilty (until proven guilty) of being potential terrorists or if a blogger denounces Islam as being particularly oppressive to women, a curious person might ask if it's true. She might be inspired by her curiosity to gather information about Islam—to visit a library or a mosque (or a library in a mosque), to read about Islam, and to meet Muslims. Such curiosity would provide her with knowledge, and if she would pay attention to what she has learned, she would become wise and her wisdom would have the potential to help transform the world. At the very least, she might transform herself.

I find that when I interact with my fellow Christians—when I talk with folk, when I argue with "friends" on social media, when I read what Christians are writing, or when I hear what they are saying from their pulpits—I am, with regrettable regularity, overcome with the urge to cringe.

Far too many of my coreligionists lack even the most basic curiosity necessary for the questioning of assumptions—not just about Islam, but about any number of important topics. Too few Christians care to ask, for example, why a scientist might have a problem reading the first chapter of Genesis as a scientific textbook. Such Christians don't doubt the conclusions of those who question the science of climate change. If a pastor declares that IUDs induce abortions by preventing fertilized eggs from implanting in the womb, they don't think through the implications of that belief in light of science, which tells us that, in fact, *most* fertilized eggs don't implant. When a government acts with urgency to shore up the finances of failing banks but is lethargic in its efforts to help homeowners with underwater mortgages or to rescue recent graduates swimming in a riptide of student debt, few Christians are curious enough to ask if there may be a better, more just way to organize the national economy.

Now here's where things get political and messy: the Christian lack of curiosity and disinterest in—even distain for—the work of gathering empirical knowledge is hugely profitable. Those who make money by selling weapons to the United States and its allies love the American Christian fear of Islam, because when we fear Muslims, we are more likely to buy bombs and the airplanes that convey those bombs to targets in the Muslim world. Corporations getting rich by selling us fossil fuels have done a great job of harnessing the Christian disinclination to learn in the ways that lead to wisdom.

They've used our suspicion of science, rooted in our rejection of evolution, to gain political support for the notion that global warming is some kind of communist plot. Retailers like Hobby Lobby have harnessed a Christian disinclination to learn reproductive biology to commercial and political advantage as they resist the implementation of the Affordable Care Act. A similar Christian disregard for economic learning has provided political cover to Wall Street power brokers as they've convinced us that debt is the path to prosperity and that whatever is good for General Motors is good for America.

This, of course, is an oversimplification, but it remains true that to be a thoughtful Christian is to practice a subversive faith. To be curious, to gather information, to attain knowledge, and to become wise is to declare one's allegiance to truth, despite what the purveyors of fear may offer for our consumption and regardless of how it may harm the bottom line of those who profit from disinformation and fear.

For those who embrace it, the humanism that inspired the Reformation remains transformative. It has the power to lead us out of fear, out of ignorance, and away from the evil that both inspire. When curiosity leads to knowledge and our knowledge leads to wisdom, then we will be living in the beloved community that is the Kingdom of God and with our thoughtfulness we will be making the world a better place for all God's children.

PART III

Living a Thoughtful Faith

8

The Thoughtfully Changing Community

Travel is fatal to prejudice, bigotry and narrow-mindedness, and many of our people need it sorely on these accounts. Broad, wholesome, charitable views of men and things can not be acquired by vegetating in one little corner of the earth all one's lifetime.

—Mark Twain[1]

"Do Christians believe Jesus was perfect?"

An interfaith group of us—Presbyterian Christians, Reform Jews, and Shiite Muslims—were sitting in an old Scottish-rite Masonic hall that our hosts had purchased and converted into a mosque in downtown Oakland, California. We had been talking about human fallibility while drinking herbal tea and munching on chips and salsa when one of the Jewish participants in the group asked for a little christological clarification.

From a purely dogmatic perspective the question is easy to answer: "of course Jesus was perfect," comes the voice of historic orthodoxy, "he was God incarnate, what else could he be?" Jesus' divine perfection is a matter of settled Church doctrine, and yet Jesus' humanity also carries the weight of settled doctrine and established Church dogma, which presents a challenge to the idea that Jesus was perfect. Imperfection is one of the marks of humanity, so if Jesus was fully human, the possibility of his perfection becomes problematic.

We'll never really know for sure, especially since the Bible is of little help. It is true that a few passages in the New Testament seem to suggest Jesus was without sin (1 Pet. 2:21–23

111

and 2 Cor. 5:21, for example), but the passages that may (or may not) describe Jesus' perfection are counterbalanced by a story found in the Gospels of Matthew and Mark in which a woman from modern-day Lebanon convinces Jesus to set aside some fairly obnoxious xenophobic attitudes around who should (and, more to the point, who should not) receive the benefits of Jesus' healing ministry. As Matthew 15:21–28 tells the story,

> Jesus . . . went away to the district of Tyre and Sidon. Just then a Canaanite woman from that region came out and started shouting, "Have mercy on me, Lord, Son of David; my daughter is tormented by a demon." But he did not answer her at all. And his disciples came and urged him, saying, "Send her away, for she keeps shouting after us." He answered, "I was sent only to the lost sheep of the house of Israel." But she came and knelt before him, saying, "Lord, help me." He answered, "It is not fair to take the children's food and throw it to the dogs." She said, "Yes, Lord, yet even the dogs eat the crumbs that fall from their masters' table." Then Jesus answered her, "Woman, great is your faith! Let it be done for you as you wish." And her daughter was healed instantly.

This is not among the Bible stories my Sunday school teachers told using flannel graphs when I was a kid in the 1970s, and as far as I know, my children never watched a Veggie Tales version of the story during their younger years in post-9/11 America. When the Common Lectionary offers this passage in its triannual cycle through the Gospels, it does so during the summer months of year A, when church attendance is low.

This is one of the Bible's difficult passages. For centuries biblical commentators have sought to preserve Jesus' immaculate reputation by suggesting Jesus' initial refusal to heal the Lebanese woman's daughter was a test of the mother's faith, but that's a bit of a stretch. The story is clear: neither Jesus, who initially ignores the woman's entreaties and then calls her daughter a dog, nor his disciples, who want Jesus to send the bothersome woman away, thought the woman or her daughter were worthy of Jesus' healing touch. This doesn't make a convincing argument in favor of Jesus being without sin. And even if the exchange between Jesus and the Gentile mother was a test, it would hardly help the case that Jesus was perfect. Anyone who would make a mother pass a test before healing her daughter is several degrees too nasty to be perfect.

There is, however, another—and I think better—way to read this story that denies neither the obvious nor the orthodox: perhaps Jesus' perfection was not measured in his being right on every point of theological doctrine but in his ability thoughtfully to repent and change when confronted with new information. In this case, the woman from Lebanon informed Jesus that his willingness to call her non-Jewish child a dog lacked kindness, and his desire to limit his healing ministry to Jews lacked compassion. When faced with this undoubtedly difficult bit of information, Jesus changed his mind and his heart, and the ability to learn, and to allow his learning to inspire change, is what identifies Jesus as divine; a similar willingness to change is a mark of the Church's righteousness (or lack thereof, as the case may be).

If Jesus' righteousness is measured not so much in his being entirely correct on every issue but in his ability to change when confronted with new information, it then follows that a person who desires to be Christlike must be willing, like Jesus, to change when presented with new information. A thoughtful Christian must embrace a faith that is able to change, for mutability is a mark of perfection, and while the Christian Church has never demonstrated perfection, it has come closest when it has proved itself able to change.

Regardless of how one reads the story of Jesus healing the child he first called a dog, it's worth pointing out that this passage probably isn't really about Jesus at all. Rather it is about the Church. Certainly Jesus is a character in the story, but as with many Jesus narratives, the Gospel writers included this memory of Jesus' ministry as a way of helping the Church address a point of contention that was dividing the community of Jesus' earliest followers. In this case, the conflict involved how and to what extent non-Jews would be welcomed into the Christian faith.

As mentioned in chapter 5, the controversy surrounding the inclusion of Gentile believers is a subject that consumes the New Testament. The earliest books of the Christian canon—1 Thessalonians, Galatians, and 1 Corinthians—all, in one way or another, deal with the issue. The last of the New Testament books to be written—Jude and 2 Peter—probably were written with non-Jewish readers in mind, so in those late books, while the Jewish/Gentile divide is not explicitly stated, it is present, and the message is clear: those whom the earliest Christians once called "dogs" now have a place at the table with the rest of God's children. The Church learned, and in response to its learning, the Church changed. This ability to learn and change is thoughtful Christianity at its best.

It would be impossible to overstate the impact of the earliest Church's thoughtful change of heart and mind on the issue of including non-Jews in the nascent movement that would become Christianity. By choosing to embrace ethnic, cultural, and national diversity, the Church was able to grow into the global religion it is today. When it comes to inclusion, the record of the Christian Church is far from perfect, but in many cases the Church has done well, and the move toward inclusion that is remembered metaphorically in the story of a Lebanese woman schooling Jesus had an indelible impact on the history of the world.

THE CHURCH REFORMED
AND ALWAYS REFORMING

If one wishes to embrace traditional notions about Jesus' perfection while, at the same time, reading the Gospels without the bother of trying to derive from them a message that simply is not found in the text, then Jesus' perfection must be manifested in his ability to learn and to change. And if the story of Jesus and the Lebanese woman really is a metaphor for the

Church's decision to be an inclusive religious body, then the Church's righteousness is measured not in its being right all of the time, but in its ability to learn and to change. This is a good thing, for if any institution ever needed to remember the importance of learning and of changing, it must be the Church, which over time has demonstrated righteousness when it has been able to learn not just from the voices of orthodoxy spoken by powerful men, but also from the voices of outsiders—such as the Lebanese woman—and from those within the community who are oppressed —such as women and slaves.

Historically, the Christian Church has proved over and over again that it has a lot to learn and that it needs to change. For this reason, many Christians—especially those in the Calvinist tradition—have embraced the idea of *ecclesia reformata, semper reformanda*, which is Latin for "the Church reformed, always reforming." The idea behind *ecclesia reformata, semper reformanda* is similar to Thomas Jefferson's belief that the United States should hold a revolution every twenty years, just to keep things fresh. For proponents of *ecclesia reformata, semper reformanda*, it's not good enough that Protestantism emerged out of a reformation half a millennium ago. Rather, the Church must keep growing, must change as the world changes.

Nowhere is this need for ongoing reformation more apparent than in the Church's relationship with Judaism. If, during the first century of the Church's life, Christians needed thoughtfully to change such that non-Jews were welcomed into the Church, for the following nineteen centuries, the Church has needed thoughtfully to change the way it has treated Jews who didn't become Christians.[2] It didn't take long before the Church went from being a Jewish sect that had a hard time welcoming non-Jews to being an overwhelmingly Gentile religion that vilified Jews. Less than a hundred years after the Church's decision to include Gentiles, Church Fathers such as Justin Martyr and Origen of Alexandria were peppering their writings with anti-Jewish invective.

Two centuries later, some seventy-five years after the Edict of Milan, which decriminalized Christianity in the Roman

Empire, and just eight years after Rome adopted Christianity as the official religion of the empire, a mob of Christians, led by their bishop, destroyed a Jewish synagogue in the city of Calinicum in modern-day Iraq. When the Roman emperor, Theodosius I, heard of the atrocity, he demanded that the bishop rebuild the synagogue at Church expense. This was entirely logical and just. At the time, Jews had the right to worship in the empire, and destroying Jewish property was illegal. Nonetheless, when Ambrose (later *Saint* Ambrose), bishop of Milan and mentor to Saint Augustine, heard of the emperor's decision he had what only can be called—anachronistically, but accurately—"a total cow."[3] "So," the bishop challenged the emperor in a letter,

> . . . the unbelieving Jews are to have a place erected out of the spoils of the Church? The patrimony acquired by the favour of Christ for Christians is to be made over to the treasury of unbelief? . . . The Jews will put this inscription of the façade of their synagogue: "The Temple of Impiety Erected Out of the Spoils of the Christians"![4]

The emperor bowed to Ambrose's criticism. The Christians in Calinicum received no punishment for razing a house of worship. The Jews were entirely on their own. Ambrose used Christianity's newfound place of power and privilege in the Roman Empire to secure not just the primacy of the Church[5] but also the relegation of Jews and of other non-Christians to such degradation that their synagogues and temples could be destroyed with impunity.

It's tempting to say Ambrose's efforts to secure special privilege for Christians at the expense of Jewish safety ended up providing legal precedence for subsequent Christian-on-Jewish violence. That may be the case, but it is more likely that the Church-and-state-sponsored anti-Semitic violence that stained the Christian legacy in the centuries following the destruction of the synagogue at Calinicum would have happened regardless of Ambrose's intervention on behalf of the Christian mob. Either way, in the Middle Ages Roman Catholic Christians did more than destroy synagogues (though they destroyed their fair share of synagogues as well). During the Crusades, Western Christian soldiers fighting under the sign of the cross slaughtered Jews along with Muslims[6] and Eastern Orthodox Christians.[7] In Europe, Christians blamed their Jewish neighbors for any number of epidemics and social ills. In 1190, English Christians, led by nobles eager to avoid paying off debts, massacred the entire Jewish population of York,[8] and in Spain, after Christians defeated Muslims in Andalucía, the Inquisition subjected Jews to unimaginable suffering for more than three hundred years.[9]

Not to be outdone by his Roman Catholic counterparts, the great German reformer Martin Luther—he of the kind face and jovial reputation—wrote an entire book (*Von den Jüden und iren Lügen* or, in English, *On the Jews and their Lies*) in which among other things he writes,

> Accordingly, it must and dare not be considered a trifling matter but a most serious one to seek counsel against this and to save our souls from the Jews, that is, from the devil and from eternal death. My advice, as I said earlier, is:
>
> First, that their synagogues be burned down, and that all who are able toss in sulphur and pitch; it would be good if someone could also throw in some hellfire. That would demonstrate to God our serious resolve and be evidence to all the world that it was in ignorance that we tolerated such houses, in which the Jews have reviled God, our dear Creator and Father, and his Son most shamefully up till now but that we have now given them their due reward.[10]

Tragically, a lot of Protestants in Europe took Luther's advice, and European Jews suffered in ways few other ethnic groups can imagine.

Time and space conspire against a full catalogue of Christian atrocities against Jews, especially in Europe; let it suffice to say that the Holocaust didn't happen in a vacuum. When, in the twentieth century, the German Nazi regime murdered some six million European Jews in less than seven years, it was the most horrific scene in an evil and tragic drama that had been playing out for centuries. The role of the Church in the drama ranged from the nodding approval of a chorus to leading villain. Historically, anti-Semitism has been Christianity's biggest and most enduring sin, and anti-Semitism has endured in the Church, in part, because for centuries Christians lacked the thoughtfulness necessary to hear the voices of outsiders and, having heard those outside voices, to change.

In the twenty-first century, however, things have gotten better thanks to a renaissance of Christian thoughtfulness. While it would be a toxic combination of naïveté and offensiveness to suggest that the sickness of anti-Semitism no longer affects the Christian Church, starting in the decades following the Second World War, the leadership of most of the world's major Christian bodies began the process of distancing itself from anti-Semitism.

Meeting in Amsterdam in 1948, the first assembly of the World Council of Churches issued a statement urging its member churches to repent of and to reject the anti-Semitism that marked the historical Church:

> We must acknowledge in all humility that too often we have failed to manifest Christian love towards our Jewish neighbours, or even a resolute will for common social justice. We have failed to fight with all our strength the age-old disorder of man which anti-Semitism represents. The churches in the past have helped to foster an image of the Jews as the sole enemies of Christ, which has contributed to anti-Semitism in the secular world. In many lands virulent anti-Semitism still threatens and in other lands the Jews are subjected to many indignities. We call upon all the churches we represent to denounce anti-Semitism, no matter what its origin, as absolutely irreconcilable with the profession and practice of the Christian faith. Anti-Semitism is sin against God and man. Only as we give convincing evidence to our Jewish neighbours that we seek for them the common rights and dignities which God wills for His children, can we come to such a meeting with them as

would make it possible to share with them the best which God has given us in Christ.[11]

In 1961, the third assembly of the World Council of Churches, meeting in New Delhi, reaffirmed the council's earlier denunciation of anti-Semitism.[12] Four years later the Roman Catholic Church, as part of reforms of the Second Vatican Council, added the considerable weight of its voice to the growing chorus of Christian churches renouncing the sin of anti-Semitism.

> True, the Jewish authorities and those who followed their lead pressed for the death of Christ; still, what happened in His passion cannot be charged against all the Jews, without distinction, then alive, nor against the Jews of today. Although the Church is the new people of God, the Jews should not be presented as rejected or accursed by God, as if this followed from the Holy Scriptures. All should see to it, then, that in catechetical work or in the preaching of the word of God they do not teach anything that does not conform to the truth of the Gospel and the spirit of Christ.
>
> Furthermore, in her rejection of every persecution against any man, the Church, mindful of the patrimony she shares with the Jews and moved not by political reasons but by the Gospel's spiritual love, decries hatred, persecutions, displays of anti-Semitism, directed against Jews at any time and by anyone.[13]

By the time the Second Vatican Council released its renunciation of anti-Semitism, the leaders of the Roman Catholic Church and, through the World Council of Churches, most of the various Eastern Orthodox churches, nearly all of the Protestant bodies in Europe, many of the Protestant churches in North America, and a growing number of Protestant churches in the developing world, had all officially rejected anti-Semitism. No one could argue that such statements have removed every vestige of anti-Semitism from the Church, but their significance cannot be overstated. Ordinary Christians, for the most part, have listened to their leaders, and today self-described anti-Semites are hard to find in the Church. (Plenty of us accuse each other of anti-Semitism, particularly when we are debating the politics of Israel and Palestine,[14] but for the most part, such accusations are merely rhetorical punches below the emotional belt. The very fact that "anti-Semite" would be used as a epithet in the modern Church is a sign of progress.) The ancient tropes that hold the Jews eternally and collectively responsible for Jesus' death and that consider Jews to be the perpetual enemies of the Church who carry out every manner of nefarious nastiness are gone, at least in polite Christian company. As incomplete as the transformation may be, the change that has transpired in the Christian Church relative to anti-Semitism is nothing short of miraculous.

LISTENING TO THE SILENCED

So how did it happen? No doubt there are sociological explanations for the Church's change on anti-Semitism, and a historical study could provide readers with pivotal moments and key figures in the process that helped Christians change their attitudes toward their Jewish neighbors, but spiritually, it seems safe to say that after witnessing the horror of the Holocaust, Christians finally started listening to the voices of their Jewish brothers and sisters in the same way that Jesus, in the fifteenth chapter of Matthew, started listening to the Lebanese woman once she confronted him with his prejudice. Like Jesus—and like its first-century Jewish-Christian forebears—the Church relented and changed its collective mind after a thoughtful consideration of voices it long had ignored.

The changes catalogued here—Jesus' willingness to see the humanity of the Lebanese woman and her daughter, the early Church's decision to embrace Gentile believers, and its collective setting aside of traditional anti-Semitism in the mid-twentieth century—all give me hope that, despite the Church's many failures, perhaps the arc of the moral universe, though long, actually does bend toward justice. Maybe the Church will participate in and be purveyors of that justice through the practice of a thoughtful faith.

It will be a long journey, however. When Jesus changed his mind after talking with the Lebanese woman, he did so as far from Jerusalem, as far from the center of religious power, as the Gospels ever placed him during his adult ministry. In order to change, Jesus had to listen to someone whose beliefs and upbringing were radically different from his own. When the Church changed its mind, deciding to include non-Jews, it did so because Christian missionaries had traveled far from home and had met people who were unlike the people in their homeland. When in the twentieth century the Church officially began the work of setting aside anti-Semitism, it did so after the horrors of the Holocaust caused Christians to journey into a new encounter with the worst expression of its ancient, deeply held hatreds and fears. These encounters with the new, the different, and the previously unexplored inspired a shift toward inclusion and acceptance. It is a shift that can be ongoing if we allow ourselves to move into and learn from new and unexplored places in the world and in our souls.

This is the work of a thoughtful faith. We must move beyond what is comfortable and familiar, meeting people who are different from us and recognizing a common humanity in their eyes. When we do this, and if we listen with genuine respect to what they have to say and are willing to explore new ideas, then perhaps the Church can keep changing for the better.

Perhaps a thoughtful journey (literally or spiritually) to Ferguson, Missouri, will help white American Christians engage in meaningful and transformative conversations about race. Maybe a trip to Iraq and Syria (even if it only is a journey mediated through the work of excellent journalism) will bring with it an understanding of the ways in which the horrors of war—together with the arms and personnel through which the horrors are inflicted—pass from conflict to conflict, from generation to generation, and will inspire thoughtful Christians to give peace a chance. Perhaps a journey to Detroit or to any of several American cities now fallen victim to capitalism's greed will open the Church's eyes to the possibility that theology and economics are linked inseparably and that a thoughtful faith can—and should—speak to both. By God's grace, perhaps the Church will journey to New Orleans and see that a city's resurrection from the devastation of a hurricane can be accompanied with wonderful music and beautiful food.

I don't know *how* the Church will change, and I don't even know *if* the Church will change. But I know the Church *can* change if the thoughtful Christians who populate the Church's pews are willing—literally or spiritually (or both)—to travel beyond the comfort of what is familiar. Certainly we never will be perfect as Jesus—in his ability to learn and change—was perfect, but transformation is inevitable if the modern Church can be like Jesus when he met the Lebanese woman. This transformation is certain if it can replicate the adventurous spirit of its earliest spiritual ancestors and if, like the twentieth-century Church, it can travel into the shadows of its own sin. That potential for change gives me hope.

9

Political Engagement

The Christ who will not worship Satan to gain the world's kingdoms is followed by Christians who will worship only Christ in unity with the Lord whom he serves. And this is intolerable to all defenders of society who are content that many gods should be worshipped if only Democracy or America or Germany or the Empire receives its due, religious homage. The antagonism of modern, tolerant culture to Christ is of course often disguised because it does not call its religious practices religious. . . . Hence, the objection it voices to Christian monotheism appears in such injunctions only as that religion should be kept out of politics and business, or that Christian faith must learn to get along with other religions. What is often meant is that not only the claims of religious groups but all consideration of the claims of Christ and God should be banished from the spheres where other gods, called values, reign.

—H. Richard Niebuhr[1]

"But, ah, why are you going to France?"

An Israeli customs agent was holding my passport and my travel itinerary, glaring at me, and her question confused me. Admittedly, it had been a long journey from San José to Tel Aviv by way of Los Angeles and Atlanta, and customs officials at Ben Gurion International Airport are notorious interrogators, so a certain measure of befuddlement on my part was to be expected, but who needs a reason to go to France?

I explained my travel plans: I was on my way to visit the Church of the Holy Sepulcher in Jerusalem; after a few days in Israel I would travel to Córdoba in Spain by way of the South of France. I was writing a book on the relationship between Christianity and Islam, and my itinerary, though admittedly erratic, was consistent with the research I wanted to do for my book. Well, that's not entirely true. Jerusalem and Córdoba both are cities rich in the history of encounters between Islam and Christianity. The South of France was a stretch bookwise, but there it was, right on the way from Judea to Andalucía, waiting for me to stop in for a visit. So I decided to go to France—just for a few days.[2]

My interlocutor, the woman who stood, holding my passport, between me and the City of God, dropped her eyes to half-mast and asked me if I was married. When she heard that I was, she clenched her jaw and glared at me. "You go to France," she said, "and how come you're not bringing your wife?!"

She sent me to her superior for further interrogation and inspection. The superior marked my passport, and as a result, soldiers, police, and sundry security personnel subjected me to extra interrogation and inspection everywhere I went in Israel. While visiting places I had learned about in Sunday school, I got strangely used to watching as young women bedecked with lethal weapons poked around in my luggage, sometimes sending the most private bits of my used laundry down onto the sacred dust of the Holy Land. "It's for your own good," these women told me each time I bent down to retrieve a pair of boxer shorts. "This is how we catch terrorists."

During my visit to Israel, I expected to encounter harsh scrutiny because I am a progressive Protestant pastor who believes Palestinians suffer undue affliction under Israel's policies of occupation and settlement. I did not, however, expect to endure the psychological trials of extended questioning nor the indignity of frequent and complete searches of my luggage just because I am the kind of unromantic, chowder-headed cad who goes off to France without his wife.[3]

In the pantheon of polarizing political issues, few debates have the potential to cause more division or to elicit more vitriol than those that surround the Holy Land. To the uninitiated, this can seem counterintuitive, because the demands of both sides of the conflict in Israel/Palestine can be distilled into fairly simple and seemingly manageable asks. Jewish Israelis do not want to be targets of Palestinian terror. Palestinian aspirations are a little more complex but no less reasonable. Palestinians want Israelis to stop occupying their land, stop ripping up orchards, stop building settlements and roads in Palestinian territory, stop knocking down Palestinian homes, stop building walls that separate Palestinians from their water and their farms and their families, and stop setting up arbitrary roadblocks that limit movement in Palestinian territory. The Palestinians, in short, want the dignity of freedom and independence. Achieving these apparently noncontradictory goals is complicated, however, by the weight of history, by the pitfalls of prejudice and tribalism, and by the pressures of contemporary politics.

When I traveled to Israel/Palestine I wanted the trip to be nonpolitical. In 2004 the denomination in which I am a member, the Presbyterian Church (U.S.A.), began the process of divesting from multinational corporations who profit from violence in the region. When we did, the blowback from pro-Israel individuals and organizations was epic. The conservative pundit Dennis Prager said we were worse than Nazis.[4] Writing for the *Los Angeles Times*, Harvard law professor Alan Dershowitz called the Presbyterian Church "immoral, sinful, and bigoted."[5] In response to the vitriol, I helped to organize a Jewish-Presbyterian dialogue group for the purpose of working out our differences. It didn't work. If anything, the rhetoric got more heated and more personal, and I got burned out.

As a form of finding spiritual renewal, I decided to be intentional about avoiding politics in the Holy Land. My plan was to spend a day or two in Jerusalem researching the relationship between Christianity and Islam before heading north to the Sea of Galilee, where I was going to read the Gospels sitting on a beach chair with my feet in the water of the lake. Then I was going to France, but in a country where even making plans for a solo journey to so romantic a destination can raise suspicions, politics are unavoidable. Everywhere I went I was reminded of the conflicts that deepen divisions between the people living in the place the children of Abraham call holy and that threaten to rend churches and families and friendships on the far side of the globe.

Israeli security is what it is because of the politics, and the inconveniences I endured as a result of my trip to France paled in comparison to what Palestinians endure every day for reasons even more arbitrary. When I interviewed the keeper of the doors of the Church of the Holy Sepulcher, we met in his home, which has been in the family for untold generations. The house was starting to get dilapidated but could not be repaired because, thanks to politics, it is difficult and expensive for Arab Israelis living in Jerusalem to get permits to fix their houses. When I went to Bethlehem, I crossed through a wall that, in the name of security and in response to political realities, the government of Israel has built deep in Palestinian territory, such that it divides families and communities, separates farmers from their land, and puts control of Palestinian water supplies entirely in the hands of Israel. Because of regional politics and because of all the countless ways Israel feels threatened by neighboring nations, when I rode Israeli busses from Jerusalem to the Sea of Galilee I could not find a seat that was not next to someone carrying an assault rifle.

Now if you happen to be a supporter of Israel—someone who, while regretting any difficulty Palestinians face, is generally supportive of the security measures Israel determines it must take to protect itself, and if you feel as if I've presented a rather one-sided portrayal of my time in the Holy Land—stay with me. I'm actually trying to make you squirm and fidget, just a little bit, because anytime Christians delve into politics (especially when said Christian comes in the form of a pastor writing a book for a denominationally affiliated publishing house), someone will get upset. Sometimes it gets personal and sometimes it gets destructive. Whole congregations have split, shriveled, or died over politics, which raises the question: Should Christians be political activists in the first place? Should we speak out on issues like those that surround Israel/Palestine, knowing full well that in so doing we will alienate a significant portion of the population, sending them out of our congregations to places where their dissent will feel more welcome (which may be another church but, more likely, will be a leisurely cup of coffee, a nice breakfast, and the Sunday *New York Times*)? Should I, as a writer, jeopardize the sales of this book by offering up even a gentle critique of Israel's policies when I know that a significant portion of my readers will take offense?

Who wants to get dressed for church or shell out eighteen hard-earned dollars for a book, only to be subjected to a political rant with which he or she disagrees? And who wants to subject others to the bits of our political doctrines that may cause offense even if they are of righteous origin?

It is tempting to say that a thoughtful Christian should hover in Zen-like detachment above the discord of political acrimony. This is especially true in the United States, where most of us see great value in the separation of church and state, which a lot of us interpret to mean that, as people of faith, we should go about the work of saving souls, and dispensing charity is fine, so long as we stick to feeding people and don't ask why they are hungry and don't get too serious about doing anything to change the societal structures that keep people poor.

It's tempting further to embrace the idea that when politics simply cannot be avoided, the thoughtful Christian should, with fair-minded equanimity, embrace all sides, seeing the wisdom and goodness of various points of view and then finding balance at the fulcrum of truth that surely must reside at a place equidistant from every extreme. After all, who wants to be like Jerry Falwell, or Pat Robertson, or those kooks from Kansas who show up with homophobic signs every time a high school drama club performs *The Laramie Project*? And who, for that matter, wants to be like the left-wing analogue of Falwell, Robertson, and Westboro Baptist Church? (That there *is* no left-wing analogue to the Christian right[6] doesn't really matter; our commitment to centrism is strong enough that we can create an imaginary pole to match the extreme right.) American Christians adore middle ground.

Christians—especially in their various Protestant manifestations—are, by nature and training, people who value evangelism. We want to see our churches grow, and we have a keen awareness of how hard it can be to grow congregations when communities are in upheaval stoked by pastors and other leaders unable to keep their politics personal. In the last forty years, as membership in mainline denominations has atrophied, an industry of church-growth experts has grown up, promising—through books and videos, consultants and training seminars—to fix what's broken in the Church and to restore the size and institutional stability of the once formidable American Church. The church health and growth industry has yielded a wide variety of suggestions—from better signage to rock-and-roll music in worship—and some of the ideas are quite good (though none, to my knowledge, has had an appreciable effect on stopping the numerical decline of American Christianity), but never has anyone connected to the Church health and growth industry suggested that congregations need more politics. The preaching of politics is bad for church business.

THE CIVIL RIGHTS MOVEMENT

It's easy—especially for contemporary Christians—to imagine that if a group of outspoken, hyperpolitical, out-of-town Christian activists showed up to address a national issue with a profound local impact in a community where we lived, we might ask our out-of-town guests to rest easy for a while, to moderate their rhetoric, and to listen to what local leadership already was doing (successfully in some cases) to address the issue. We might point out that, by their presence, the activists were causing division that actually was making things worse locally. We might even applaud if a group of interfaith religious leaders from our area wrote a letter to the pastor organizing the outside activists, calling for unity, and asking the pastor to respect the local process.

This is exactly what happened in Birmingham, Alabama, in 1963 when civil rights activists, led by the Rev. Dr. Martin Luther King Jr., began demonstrating and organizing in the community. The slow, locally led progress toward legal equality in Birmingham was derailed by the better organized, faster moving, more effective work that King's organization brought to town. For a while, things got chaotic in Birmingham, and in response, a group of local white religious leaders—bishops,

pastors, and a rabbi—published an open letter in the local
newspaper that, in part, read,

> . . . we are now confronted by a series of demonstrations
> by some of our Negro citizens, directed and led in part by
> outsiders. We recognize the natural impatience of people
> who feel that their hopes are slow in being realized. But
> we are convinced that these demonstrations are unwise and
> untimely.
>
> We agree rather with certain local Negro leadership
> which has called for honest and open negotiation of racial
> issues in our area. And we believe this kind of facing of
> issues can best be accomplished by citizens of our own met-
> ropolitan area, white and Negro, meeting with their knowl-
> edge and experience of the local situation. All of us need
> to face that responsibility and find proper channels for its
> accomplishment.
>
> Just as we formerly pointed out that "hatred and violence
> have no sanction in our religious and political traditions,"
> we also point out that such actions as incite to hatred and
> violence, however technically peaceful those actions may
> be, have not contributed to the resolution of our local prob-
> lems. We do not believe that these days of new hope are
> days when extreme measures are justified in Birmingham.[7]

Martin Luther King read the clergymen's public statement
while in jail (he'd been arrested for organizing a protest without a parade permit) and, in response, he penned a letter that
is among the most significant treatises on the importance of
mixing religion and politics ever written. In his "Letter from
a Birmingham Jail," King expressed his dissatisfaction with
the political moderation practiced by so many white people
of faith using language that should trouble any contemporary
Christian who has, in the name of balance or inclusion, refused
to mix politics and religion.

> I have almost reached the regrettable conclusion that the
> Negro's great stumbling block in his stride toward freedom
> is not the White Citizen's Counciler or the Ku Klux Klan-
> ner, but the white moderate, who is more devoted to "order"

than to justice; who prefers a negative peace which is the absence of tension to a positive peace which is the presence of justice; who constantly says: "I agree with you in the goal you seek, but I cannot agree with your methods of direct action"; who paternalistically believes he can set the time-table for another man's freedom; who lives by a mythical concept of time and who constantly advises the Negro to wait for a "more convenient season." Shallow understanding from people of good will is more frustrating than absolute misunderstanding from people of ill will. Lukewarm accep-tance is much more bewildering than outright rejection.[8]

There are some Christians, no doubt, who, in response to King's "Letter from a Birmingham Jail," may say that that political activism—however lofty and just the goals—simply is not the vocation of the Church, which is neither equipped nor prepared to jump into the messiness of secular politics. The Church, according to this line of thought, exists to point sinners to the saving love and grace of Jesus, through which a person will be sanctified and transformed so that her social and political attitudes may eventually conform to the biblical vision of the Kingdom of Heaven. But that transformation cannot take place if the Church is engaged in political actions that scare off the very people who most need transformation. The work of the Church, therefore, is to be a strong and vibrant institution able to attract the degenerate and, with God's help, make them saints.

As attractive as the argument may be, its comeliness doesn't last under the unforgiving glare of King's analysis. King writes,

In the midst of blatant injustices inflicted upon the Negro, I have watched white churchmen stand on the sideline and mouth pious irrelevancies and sanctimonious trivialities. In the midst of a mighty struggle to rid our nation of racial and economic injustice, I have heard many ministers say: "Those are social issues, with which the gospel has no real concern." And I have watched many churches commit themselves to a completely other worldly religion which makes a strange, un-Biblical distinction between body and soul, between the sacred and the secular.[9]

It is worth noting that the American civil rights movement did not invent the concept of Christian political activism. Rather, in his "Letter from a Birmingham Jail," King synthesizes and articulates theological propositions that are as old as Christianity itself. While many Christians over the centuries—especially those who possessed power and wealth—have urged the Church to remain silent in the political realm and urged Christians to obey even the most morally bankrupt of laws, still, over the centuries, the finest theological minds have reminded people of faith that righteous citizens cannot obey the unrighteous demands of corrupt and evil worldly powers any more than the Church can claim fidelity to the Gospel if its pulpits remain silent in the face of oppression, corruption, violence, and greed.

The idea that churches—and individual Christians—should be active in transformative politics by establishing just polities and resisting immoral laws is particularly important in the tradition of Reformed Protestantism, that brand of Christianity born of the Swiss reformation under the leadership of John Calvin. Calvin and his followers affirmed the right of kings and magistrates to make, administer, and enforce laws, but they also believed earthly rulers and their policies were subject—like everyone else—to heavenly standards of morality. Meanwhile, the Reformed Protestant belief in universal human fallibility meant that human governments would forever fail to attain the heavenly moral standards to which they were subject. That ongoing failure, in turn, meant that the Church would be called to an unending project of speaking truth to power and of agitating on behalf of justice, righteousness, and the well-being of God's children. "No Protestant," to quote the great twentieth-century theologian and ecumenist Robert McAfee Brown, "who takes his or her own heritage seriously can sit on the political sidelines."[10]

If we were to expunge all politics from the Church we would be forced to rid ourselves of a "Letter from a Birmingham Jail" and most everything else Martin Luther King Jr. said, wrote, and stood for. We'd also be forced to distance ourselves from Dorothy Day, Desmond Tutu, Jim Wallis, William Sloane

Coffin, and Pope Francis. People of faith have played instrumental roles in ending slavery, in winning the right of women to vote, and in making marriage equality a reality in the United States, all because we've allowed politics to "creep" into our churches. People of faith have spoken out against wars in Vietnam and Iraq; we've opposed apartheid in South Africa and American-sponsored violence in Central America; and now many of us are speaking out on behalf of Palestinians, who suffer under Israel's illegal and often violent occupation of the West Bank and the Gaza Strip.[11]

NONVIOLENT POLITICS

After ten years, the above-mentioned Presbyterian decision to explore divesting from multinational companies who profit from the Israeli occupation of Palestinian territories resulted in the Presbyterian Church (U.S.A.)'s 2014 decision to divest from three companies: Motorola (because it supplies the Israel Defense Forces with communication technology specifically designed for operation in the West Bank), Hewlett-Packard (because it supplies biometric software used to track Palestinian civilians), and Caterpillar (because it provides the Israel Defense Forces with bulldozers designed to destroy Palestinian homes and orchards).[12]

The Presbyterian decision to divest from Motorola, Hewlett-Packard, and Caterpillar was controversial. The vote on the floor of the General Assembly, which is the biannual meeting of the denomination's highest governing body, was close, and the move generated some significant (and predictable) blowback from those inclined to support Israeli policies. The American Jewish Committee deemed the Presbyterian Church (U.S.A.) motivated by hatred of Israel, and the Israeli embassy declared the action shameful.[13] The Anti-Defamation League accused Presbyterian leadership of having "fomented an atmosphere of open hostility to Israel in the church,"[14] and Israeli Prime Minister Benjamin Netanyahu, speaking on NBC's *Meet the*

Press, said the Presbyterian Church's decision to divest from Motorola, Hewlett-Packard, and Caterpillar "should trouble all people of conscience and morality because it's so disgraceful."[15]

Like many Presbyterians, I supported the Presbyterian divestment from Motorola, Hewlett-Packard, and Caterpillar because I don't believe the Presbyterian Church should profit from violence of any kind, and personally, I don't want my pension invested in companies that profit from violence of any kind. If any publicly traded companies are profiting from violence perpetrated by Palestinians against Israel, I want to be divested from those companies as well. When the violence from which a person or an institution is divesting is state-sponsored, that divestment becomes, inherently, a political act, and within weeks of the Presbyterian decision to divest from Motorola, Hewlett-Packard, and Caterpillar, the urgency and necessity of such political actions became clear.

On June 12, 2014, kidnappers—apparently affiliated with Hamas—abducted and later murdered three teenaged yeshiva students who were hitchhiking in the West Bank.[16] Then, on July 2, 2014, police found the body of a Palestinian teen who, in what seems to have been an act of revenge, had been burned alive.[17] Before long the situation got desperately out of control. Militants in the Hamas-led Gaza Strip were firing rockets into Israel, and Israel responded by attacking the Gaza Strip with unimaginable ferocity. Regrettably, both sides targeted civilians, but Israel did so with greater efficiency, targeting civilian homes, hospitals, and schools that were being used as refugee shelters. After a month of fighting, the United Nations' Office for the Coordination of Humanitarian Affairs reported 67 Israeli dead (3 of whom were civilians), and 1,814 Palestinian dead (1,312 of whom were civilians, 408 of whom were children, and 214 of whom were women). In addition, more than half a million Palestinians were displaced and more than 65,000 Palestinians permanently lost their homes.[18]

The violence did not happen in a vacuum. The Gaza Strip so devastated by Israeli military might during the summer of 2014 already was a place of extreme poverty. For years the people of Gaza suffered under Israeli occupation and siege. An Israeli economic blockade of Gaza placed limits on the kinds of goods and services denizens of Gaza could enjoy. Israeli restrictions on farming and fishing in Gaza made the population reliant on outside food aid that, as a result of the Israeli blockade, frequently was slow to arrive. An embargo against building materials meant that Gaza was unable fully to rebuild from the assaults Israel launched against the territory in 2009 and 2012.[19]

For their part, Palestinian militants in Gaza have sent thousands of rockets into Israel over the last decade. Few of these attacks have caused actual damage, but the attacks are, nonetheless, heinous violations of all that is decent (to say nothing of breaking international law), and they come in the context of decades of terrorist attacks directed at Israel. The whole situation is a bloody mess, and if there is one thing upon which good-willed people on both sides of the debate *should* be able to agree it is this: violence has done nothing to solve anything in the Holy Land. This is why thoughtful Christians must engage the situation through nonviolent, political (as opposed to violent military) processes.

Divestment is a nonviolent response to an extremely violent situation. The Israeli occupation of Palestine is sucking the life out of both nations, and it is having a detrimental effect on countries in the region and across the world as well. The last thing we need in the Holy Land is more violence, more weapons, or more logistical support for violence on either side. Divestment is an effective way to work toward an end without killing anyone.

When Presbyterians and other like-minded people of faith choose to engage politically by joining various economic boycotts, the question should not be "why?" The question should be "why not?" Why would the Presbyterian Church *not* want to join a political movement that seeks peace in Jesus' homeland using economic boycotts, a method that is both effective and nonviolent? Why would the Presbyterian Church *not* want to join Christian, Muslim, and Jewish friends in a process that seeks to remove weapons and military systems from a region torn apart by decades of war? Violence has done nothing to foster peace between Israeli Jews and Palestinians. Why *not* use political activism that gives peace a chance to diminish the violence?

NECESSARY DISCOMFORT

The problem, of course, is this: as surely as some Christians feel divestment from companies that profit from the Israeli occupation of Palestinian lands (and other similar nonviolent political action on behalf of beleaguered Palestinians) is both merited and necessary, other Christians—perhaps sitting in the same pew—will believe with equal conviction that such activity downplays Palestinian culpability in the conflict, demonizes Israel, and degrades Israel's ability to defend itself. Given the fact that so many Jews around the world have strong familial, spiritual, and emotional ties to Israel, many Christians also fear political action on behalf of Palestinians will harm interfaith relationships (to say nothing of individual friendships and familial ties).

One cannot overstate the extent to which political activity in churches can cause discomfort in denominations, in congregations, and between Christian friends and loved ones, but there is nothing within the biblical witness or the Christian tradition that suggests avoiding discomfort is virtuous, moral, or Christlike behavior. In fact, many of the greatest and most celebrated saints are revered precisely because they were willing to engage the human condition at its most uncomfortable places.

If the confluence of religion and politics makes us uncomfortable, perhaps, rather than avoiding the discomfort, a thoughtful Christian may consider listening to the discomfort, for sometimes the Spirit speaks through discomfort. If this chapter's embrace of moderate, nonviolent, pro-Palestinian (though not, I think, truly anti-Israeli) politics causes discomfort, perhaps the Spirit is calling the discomforted to change their minds. Maybe the Spirit is calling the discomforted to try to articulate the realities of Middle Eastern politics in such a way that people like me no longer will support divestment from companies that profit from Israel's occupation of Palestinian territory. Either way, I've never known the Spirit to call the thoughtful Christian to a selective faith. There is no part of life that is exempt from the demands of righteousness and justice and mercy and grace. This means that, for people of faith, politics are as unavoidable in the United States as they are in the Holy Land. It means we must speak out and be active and work for change, even when we'd rather stand on the sidelines, singing *kum ba yah*.

It's inconvenient, because inaction always has been easier than conflict, but as I study history, I am most proud to call myself a Christian when I hear stories of men and women of faith who have taken action, who have spoken out on controversial issues, and who have given of themselves to change the world even when the cost was great. And I want to believe the best days of the Christian Church lie in the future. Those days will come when Christians rise up en masse to make our society more caring, more just, more peaceful, when our influence at home will help to keep children healthy, well-educated, and well-fed, and when our activism overseas will play a part in doing things like establishing a just peace in the Holy Land.

If we're going to get there, we will have to push and pull and stretch in ways that will be uncomfortable. Sometimes we'll push and pull and stretch in different directions, but I trust the Spirit to lead us safely on, to use us and to inspire us to do great things, and to bring us at the last into the beloved community we all long to see made manifest on earth.

10

Creative Embodiment

We lay foundations that will need further development.
We provide yeast that produces far beyond our capabilities.
We cannot do everything, and there is a sense of liberation in
    realizing that.
This enables us to do something, and to do it very well.
It may be incomplete, but it is a beginning, a step along the
    way, an opportunity for the Lord's grace to enter and do
    the rest.
We may never see the end results, but that is the difference
    between the master builder and the worker.
We are workers, not master builders; ministers, not messiahs.
We are prophets of a future not our own.
        —From a prayer written by Bishop Ken Untener of
        Saginaw, Michigan, but usually attributed to
        Archbishop Oscar Romero of El Salvador[1]

During the summer of 1524, the Zurich city council directed workers to remove all artistic expressions from the city's seven churches. The wrecking crews tore down paintings, walled up organs, smashed statues, and removed stained glass windows until what remained were worship spaces that—though still beautiful in their austerity—were somewhat spare, especially in relation to church buildings in other parts of Europe, which were just getting ready to embrace the ornate gaudiness of Baroque architecture.[2]

The destruction of art in Zurich came at the prompting of Huldrych Zwingli, the theologian, pastor, and former Roman Catholic priest who led the Protestant reformation in northern Switzerland. Zwingli was convinced Christian worship should be simple and unadorned by anything not found in or directed by Scripture, and his desire to destroy what he found unbiblical was not limited to ecclesiastical ornamentation. This is the same Zwingli we met in chapter 6; that Zwingli also prompted the martyrdom of Swiss Anabaptists is clear evidence that his desire to destroy art was not his greatest sin, but still, the iconoclastic zealotry of Swiss German Protestants caused the destruction of untold works of great cultural significance.

While no one can endorse the slaughter of Anabaptists, a person could make a case in defense of removing art from churches. After all, the prohibition against making "graven images" is catalogued among the Big Ten (by which I don't mean the athletic conference of universities around the Great Lakes), and stylistic simplicity has been an aesthetic hallmark of many Protestant traditions. There are exceptions, of course—Anglicans aren't particularly known for shunning ecclesiastical ostentation—but from whitewashed clapboard Congregationalist churches in New England to storefront Salvation Army outposts in the inner city, most Protestants have embraced simplicity. This was as true for Calvinists in Scotland whose church architecture reflects Zwinglian sensibilities as it is true for modern, nondenominational megachurches[3] who prefer the utility of theater-like worship spaces—many of which have a warehouse vibe—to the beauty of gilded sanctuaries. Usually this is not a financial decision—the audiovisual systems in many large churches can cost as much as stained glass windows—rather, the choice reflects the deep Protestant roots to which the "independent" churches are connected.

This is not to say that Protestantism has been entirely devoid of art. Johann Sebastian Bach was a Protestant, for example (though as a Lutheran he did not worship among the kind of Protestants who, a hundred years before his birth, were destroying organs and smashing stained glass) and many modern Protestant congregations—including many of the warehouse/theater variety—are vibrant artistic communities. But the historical tendency among many Protestants to be suspicious of artistic endeavors, particularly in the worship space, should prompt the thoughtful Christian to ask if there is at least some virtue to Zwingli's vision for an artless church.

The short answer is no, but since short answers make for dissatisfying reading, let's take a look at one of the twentieth century's finest books on the subject of art and faith, *The Mind of the Maker* by Dorothy L. Sayers. Most people know Sayers as a writer of mystery novels featuring the debonair detective Lord Peter Wimsey, but she also was a brilliant scholar. She was among the first women to earn an advanced degree from Oxford, her translation of the *Divine Comedy* is among the most popular English translations of Dante's poem, and she was an essayist who wrote on a broad range of topics. Sayers was friendly with C. S. Lewis and J. R. R. Tolkien, though she was not—as many assume—a member of the Inklings, the literary circle that gathered at The Eagle and Child in Oxford to drink and swap stories (see chap. 6). Probably she never joined the Inklings because they were something of an old boy's club and she was a feminist. Perhaps she wasn't asked to join, or maybe she had no desire to be in the company of drunken male colleagues. Besides, it's likely she was far too busy.

In *The Mind of the Maker*, Sayers suggests that when the first chapter of Genesis describes humans as being made in the image of God, it is saying that we, like God, are creators. This means that when we are engaged in creative pursuits, when we are artists—when we paint, sculpt, dance, play music, write poetry, or, for that matter, when we approach any part of life with creativity and ingenuity—we are expressing the image of God in which we are created.[4]

For many Christians, this is something of a revolutionary idea. Most Christians do a good job of understanding all the ways a person can make spiritual connections with the Divine through prayer, corporate worship, Bible study, singing along with old Amy Grant cassettes (extra credit for *Age to Age*),[5] and adopting the right sorts of beliefs about God. Christians also have long understood the importance of doing good works— of dispensing charity and of working for justice and peace. Few of us realize, however (particularly if we're Protestants), that one way to draw close to God, one way to experience a connection to the Divine, is to be an artist. To create beauty through music or words or with pigments on paper or canvas, with sculpture or architecture or any other creative pursuit, is to know God by seeing God's image alive in ourselves.

NONARTISTIC CREATIVITY

So three cheers for the arts, but what of those who cannot draw, sculpt, play musical instruments, or dance? Can those who are not inclined to artistic pursuits experience the spiritual joy of finding God by expressing God's image through creativity?

The answer is yes. Yes, because everyone is capable of creative expression. It may not be what we understand to be traditionally artistic creativity (though just about everyone has the capacity to do some kind of art, even if it's not museum quality), but anyone who ever has a problem to solve or a solution to provide, anyone who builds anything or offers a service has the opportunity to be creative. When we do any work well, with intelligence and love, we are being creative and we are giving life and expression to the image of God alive in us. As people of faith we need to be more intentional about encouraging creativity in ourselves and in our communities. This is as true for actors and designers as it is for auto mechanics and carpenters.

In her essay "Why Work," Dorothy Sayers writes,

> The Church's approach to an intelligent carpenter is usually confined to exhorting him not to be drunk and disorderly in his leisure hours, and to come to church on Sundays. What the Church should be telling him is this: that the very first demand that his religion makes upon him is that he should make good tables. Church by all means, and decent forms of amusement, certainly—but what use is all that if in the very center of his life and occupation he is insulting God with bad carpentry? No crooked table legs or ill-fitting drawers ever came out of the carpenter's shop at Nazareth. Nor, if they did, could anyone believe that they were made by the same hand that made Heaven and earth.[6]

This, by the way, is an excellent description of the Calvinist work ethic. The sociologist Max Weber said Calvinists work hard because we want our successes to serve as proof we are among God's elect and are, therefore, future denizens of heaven. Weber's hypothesis may or may not be accurate, but I suspect John Calvin would describe the Calvinist work ethic much in the same way Sayers describes the work of an intelligent carpenter. We do good work; we are creative, intelligent, generous, and loving in all our endeavors because to work well, to be creative in all we do, is to glorify God.

So we derive great spiritual benefits from our creativity, from living out the image of God in which we are created. Creativity helps us to be fully human and therefore somewhat divine whether we are paving roads or writing plays, but creativity is not just a spiritual luxury, like meditation. It's not just something we can do as a way of taking care of ourselves by pampering our souls. In reality, the world around us is crying out for creativity.

THE INTELLIGENT CARPENTER IN THE LAND OF THE SANDINISTAS

In the spring of 1987, my brother Morgan Daniel and our friend Patrick Rickon bought Schwinn mountain bikes, loaded them up with camping equipment, and rode south to Mexico from our hometown on California's north coast. Ten months earlier, Morgan had dropped out of college after completing one year. During the spring break of his freshman year, he'd spent a week doing short-term mission work in Ensenada, Baja California, and it changed him. Having seen poverty up close, Morgan wasn't ready to return to life in the United States without first exploring the ways in which people in other countries live. He returned home from college and joined Patrick—his lifelong best friend—on a construction crew building houses for a local contractor. Together, the pair saved money and made plans to return to Mexico.

After pedaling to the U.S./Mexico border, they spent three and a half months living in and working at an orphanage in Tijuana. Then, after hearing of a "real" Mexico that existed further south, they exchanged their bikes for bus tickets and headed in the general direction of the Yucatán peninsula. Once in Mexico's south, they kept going, eventually landing—by way of Belize—at a language school in Antigua, Guatemala.

Now better able to speak Spanish, Morgan and Patrick returned for a time to the orphanage in Tijuana, but Central America had captured their imaginations, and when a group of much older adults from our hometown invited Morgan and Patrick to join them on a Habitat for Humanity project in Nicaragua, they jumped at the opportunity. Because plane tickets cost more than their entire eight-month sojourn south of the U.S./Mexico border, Morgan and Patrick got back on busses and headed south to Nicaragua, a country which, at the time, was embroiled in a civil war whose antagonists fought as proxies for Cold War superpowers eager to gain (on the one hand) or maintain (on the other) power and influence in Central America.

In 1979, after eighteen years of revolution, members of the *Frente Sandinista de Liberación Nacional* (Sandinista National Liberation Front), or the Sandinistas, overthrew the regime of Nicaraguan dictator Anastasio Somoza Debayle, bringing an end to more than four decades of rule by the U.S.-backed Somoza family, who governed the Central American nation with a nefarious blend of nepotism, violence, and graft. The Sandinistas also overthrew a dictatorship that, for the United States, had been a reliable Cold War ally. Before long the United States was funding a counterrevolution in Nicaragua. The war was ugly. Both sides drew international condemnation for human rights abuses, and when the United States Congress decided, in 1984, to defund American support for Nicaraguan counterrevolutionaries (or Contras), the administration of President Ronald Reagan searched outside of legal boxes to fund the Contra cause. Such nontraditional financing included the proceeds from illegal arms sales to Iran and from drug smuggling operations that, with CIA knowledge and cooperation, brought cocaine from Colombia, through Central America, and to the streets of Los Angeles, where it was sold as crack.[7]

So Nicaragua may not have been the safest or sanest place for a couple of rural northern Californian twenty-year-olds to visit, arriving, as they did, by bus through Contra-controlled territory in Honduras and northern Nicaragua, but twenty-year-olds believe themselves to be immortal, and in the late eighties, Nicaragua was a magnet for idealistic, left-leaning travelers drawn to the Sandinista program of social reform, including—and perhaps especially—their educational agenda, which aimed to make Nicaragua the most literate nation in Latin America.

After passing unscathed through war zones in Guatemala and Nicaragua, Patrick and Morgan joined the Habitat for Humanity group and built houses along the shores of Lago de Apanas, and in the process they impressed the group's leader, a clergyman named Todd Evans. They returned home to northern California, went back to working construction jobs, and assumed their travels were over, but Todd Evans remembered Patrick's skills as a builder, and when one of the Habitat volunteers offered to donate a jacuzzi pump for a potable water project in the community where the Habitat group had built houses, Todd suggested Patrick should lead the work of installing the water system.

Patrick accepted the job, but this time he had to travel alone. My brother, his longtime traveling companion, had fallen in love and was engaged to be married. So Patrick flew to Nicaragua by himself. The water project was more or less a fiasco—it turns out that a jacuzzi pump cannot supply water to a village—but while working on the water project, Patrick made friends with the operator of Habitat for Humanity's sawmill, which produced lumber for Habitat's projects in Nicaragua. Patrick took scrap lumber from the mill and used it to make furniture for his small house, and that gave the millwright an idea: perhaps Patrick could design and build school desks, which, in rural Nicaragua, were in short supply.

As mentioned above, during the era of Sandinista rule, the Nicaraguan government established policies that attempted to improve literacy among the country's rural population. These efforts at education appealed to progressive idealists in Europe and North America who came to Nicaragua with great energy and enthusiasm. They built wonderful school buildings but forgot to supply furniture for those schools, thus rendering the fine schoolhouses almost useless in the project of educating rural Nicaragua.

Patrick designed and built a school's worth of desks. He and his millwright friend loaded those desks onto rowboats to convey the desks to a school on the far side of Lago de Apanos. The crossing was tough. The wind was against them, and sometimes it felt as if they wouldn't make it, but when the load of desks finally made the far side of the lake, a crowd of schoolchildren met them on the shore, swimming out to the boats to grab the furniture that would make their school functional. The locals threw a party, and they danced into the night. Patrick realized he was exactly where he wanted to be, and he has lived in Nicaragua ever since.

The desk project grew. Before long, Patrick was teaching others how to build desks and, in the process, instructing Nicaraguan peasants in carpentry skills. In time, all of the nearby schools were outfitted with desks, and so Patrick welcomed work groups from northern California to build yet more schools in which to put more desks. Together with Todd Evans, the leader of the Habitat for Humanity work group from northern California, and the man who originally invited Patrick and Morgan to join them in Nicaragua, Patrick started an organization called Seeds of Learning. This organization supported Patrick's work with fundraising and built an institutional framework that strengthened Patrick's work and helped recruit volunteers to join the work in Nicaragua.

Seeds of Learning grew. Patrick married a teacher and, together with his Nicaraguan bride, he established an educational resource center that provides instructional support for local students and helps to train teachers from all around Nicaragua. Following the success of the first learning resource center, Patrick and his coworkers established two more centers in Nicaragua and in El Salvador. Today, Seeds of Learning is working throughout Nicaragua and El Salvador, supporting local efforts to improve education in Central America. Nearly a quarter of a century after Patrick built his first school desk, the Seeds of Learning website reports,

> Since its inception in 1991, Seeds of Learning has constructed or remodeled 152 classrooms in 55 communities; built and repaired several thousand school desks and furnishings; developed three Learning Resource Centers; awarded scholarships to over 1064 primary, high school, and university students; supported literacy and adult education programs in over 20 rural communities; and sent over 2,440 work group volunteers to Central America. SOL serves over 300 students a day in the Learning Resource Centers, equipped with 3,500 books for students and teachers, and offers classes in dance, music, sewing, embroidery, crafts, English and computer basics, and tutoring.[8]

With the exception of a brief childhood trip to Oregon, Patrick had never left California prior to his Central American journeys with my brother. Not having found academic success in high school, he didn't attend college. At age nineteen, when his travels in Central America began, few of the people who knew Patrick would have predicted he would one day help to start a multinational nongovernmental organization that works in the field of educational development. Yet Patrick was able to do wonderful and unexpected things with his life because Patrick is a thoughtful Christian whose mind is gifted with an extra measure of creativity.

In October of 2014, I caught up with Patrick on Skype to double-check the details of his story and to ask him if he thought creativity played a role in the formation of his life and work. In response, he told me about playing bass in my brother's garage band (a barn band, actually—we didn't have a garage). When my brother wanted to start a band, none of his friends played the right kinds of instruments, so he talked our neighbor, Wayne, into playing the drums, and Patrick into playing the bass. Morgan covered keyboards, guitar, and vocals. Morgan had musical training, Patrick and Wayne, not so much. They made it up as they went along and ended up sounding really good.[9]

Playing the bass gave Patrick a sense of confidence that he carried with him like a tool. Whether it was riding a bike from behind California's Redwood Curtain to Mexico or traveling by bus through war-torn, third-world nations or building school desks or starting a learning resource center, he remembers: "If I can learn to play the bass, I can do this."

Motivated by his experience as a garage band bassist, Patrick has sought to make creativity part of every Seeds of Learning educational project. The Learning Resource Center teaches music and other arts to students, and it encourages teachers to bring creativity into the schools of rural Central America because, from his own experience, he knows the value of a creative mind.

"Sometimes I feel like a plastic bag full of water," he told me, "and when opportunities for creativity come along, they poke a hole in the bag, and the water pours out and waters the ground, and the earth blossoms."

CREATIVITY, CLOSER TO HOME

While traveling to Nicaragua in the middle of a revolution and using one's creativity to address deficiencies in the local educational system is a good thing to do, one need not take such drastic measures to find places where thoughtful Christian creativity can be used to solve problems. Between 1997 and 2014 I lived in San José, California, in the heart of Silicon Valley at a time when the high-tech industry was generating more money than any other valley ever produced in a similar timespan in human history, yet by the time I moved north to Oakland, San José boasted the largest homeless encampment in the United States. Called "the Jungle" and situated along Coyote Creek, just south and east of San José's gleaming city center, the encampment was home to hundreds of people. While most people referred to the Jungle as an encampment, I've spent enough time in the developing world to know that the Jungle was more like a shantytown, the kind of urban slum one can find in pretty much any city in Latin America.

The Jungle wasn't the only homeless community in San José. Such settlements could be found all up and down the creeks that flow through the Santa Clara Valley and into the San Francisco Bay and likely exist under overpasses and along urban streams in just about every major American city. Something needs to be done, and I do not know what that something is. The factors that contribute to homelessness are many and they are complex, and in a region where even the most dilapidated of studio apartments rents for more than a thousand dollars a month, solutions to the challenge of homelessness can seem absolutely unattainable. This is why thoughtful Christians must foster creativity.

Solutions to homelessness are out there; we just need to think creatively until we find them. Or, to borrow an image from Patrick Rickon, we need for someone's plastic bag of creative water to be pricked. The image of God is alive in us not just when we are making art for art's sake; we encounter the image of God within us whenever we do any job well, and especially, I think, when we are creatively doing good work that helps solve problems like homelessness, poverty, educational inequality, and chronic unemployment.

There is no doubt the world needs to see the image of God manifested in the creativity of thoughtful Christians. I started writing this chapter in the summer of 2014, a time when a "surge" of unaccompanied, undocumented migrant children was making its way across the U.S./Mexico border. Most of the children in the surge were fleeing violence in Central America; many would qualify as refugees under international law.[10] Tens of thousands of children crossed the border during the time it took me to write this book, and as politicians and governmental agencies tried to figure out what to do with the children, American "patriots" protested their presence in the land of the free, with demands that the children be sent back to the violence from which they had escaped. Meanwhile, as a deep and prolonged drought in the American West threatened to bring the state of California to its knees, the state's fifth-largest newspaper, *The Orange County Register,* suggested in an editorial attacking the state's newly enacted water-use monitoring program that the lack of moisture was "largely a government-created problem looking for a government solution."[11] In another arid landscape, the Israeli military was busy bombing Gaza back to the Bronze Age, killing more than a thousand civilians, including hundreds of children. Russia was firing mortars into Ukraine, and, in Western Africa, the Ebola virus killed almost as many people in Guinea, Sierra Leone, and Liberia as the bombing had killed in Gaza.[12]

These acute issues rested on top of ongoing problems that continue to plague the United States: rampant gun violence, a lack of access to healthy food in inner cities, unemployment, a widening divide between the wealthy and the poor, intractable gridlock in Washington, educational inequality across the country, and a media more interested in Justin Bieber's Peter Pan complex than in issues of serious concern. Comedian Stephen Colbert captured the mood of the summer of 2014 when he quipped, "Things might actually be as bad as we make them sound on cable news."[13]

The summer of 2014 will be a fading memory by the time anyone other than my long-suffering wife reads these words, and by comparison, subsequent summers may be better or worse, but if progress is made on any of the issues mentioned in the preceding paragraphs (or on other issues, equally challenging, that are sure to arise), it will come as a result of creative thoughtfulness.

This is why the defunding of art and music programs in American public schools is more than just a shame. It is a social tragedy. We need to invest in programs that foster creativity, not just so the world will be filled with more beautiful and wonderful art—although that's important too—but we need to promote the arts so that the pump of our creative juices will be well-primed when we face the problems that make life difficult.

When we have lived creatively, filling our lives and our communities with beautiful objects and wonderful music; when we've written beautifully constructed sentences; when we've danced and played, surrounding ourselves with wonder; when we've worked well, facing problems with intelligence, imagination, and love; and when, with creativity, we have addressed society's ills, then we will have met God by giving expression to the divine image in which we are created. And with the creating God, we will be able to look at what we have done and say, with God, "it is good."

WINDOWS IN ZURICH

This being the final chapter of a book you have been kind enough and, at times (I'm sure), indulgent enough to read, it seems well worth ending on a positive note—something that may confirm a person's faith in Martin Luther King's assertion that the arc of the moral universe, though long, bends toward justice. For this affirmation of hope in things yet seen, we will end at the very beginning by returning to Zurich, where this chapter began.

As mentioned at the beginning of this chapter, during the summer of 1524 Zurich lost all of its stained glass windows. This destruction happened despite the fact that Huldrych Zwingli, the leader of Zurich's reformation, specifically excluded the windows in his call to destroy ecclesiastical art.[14] Passionate followers of Huldrych Zwingli went on a rampage, and in the destruction of religiously inspired art, church windows were an easy target for staffs and stones and theological indignation.

What the Zwinglian iconoclasts did not realize, however, is that stained glass also has a practical purpose. Most churches in Europe—following pagan traditions—are built with an eastern orientation so that the congregation, during morning worship, faces the rising sun. If a church has windows behind the high altar (as many do), the stained glass can help cut down the glare during morning worship. This is something the people of Zurich found out the hard way. They knocked out windows in a fit of righteous indignation and then, for the next several centuries, churchgoers in Zurich squinted their eyes, trying to see the backlit preacher if it happened to be sunny on the Lord's day. In the eighteenth century the Grossmünster church—Zurich's largest—installed curtains to block the morning sun, but that solution was kind of ugly, and it made the sanctuary dark.

Some theological convictions take centuries to mellow, but in the mid-nineteenth century church leaders relented and installed German-designed stained glass in the Grossmünster's eastern windows. These windows epitomized Victorian sensibilities, and by the Jazz Age most folks in Zurich found them embarrassingly passé. In 1933, the Grossmünster congregation commissioned the Italian artist Augusto Giacometti to design stained glass windows. The church installed these windows in the choir.[15] The windows, which are beautiful, caught the attention of the members of the second-largest church in Zurich, the Fraumünster, on the far side of the Limmat River. They also commissioned Giacometti to design a window for their sanctuary. This set up something of a stained-glass rivalry between the two churches.

In 1967, the Fraumünster commissioned Marc Chagall to create stained glass windows for its sanctuary. The Chagall windows are breathtaking and awe inspiring. They made the people of the Grossmünster a little bit jealous, and by the turn of the twenty-first century the Grossmünster congregation had had enough. It was time to find an artist would could make windows that could compete with Chagall.

Of course, no one can compete with Chagall, but the Grossmünster did find Sigmar Polke, a German artist whose windows are hauntingly stunning. Some depict biblical figures, and some make use of thin slices of agate to create psychedelic abstract images that cause the morning light to dance.

Thanks to the stained-glass smackdown, Zurich now boasts some of the most interesting and compelling church windows in Europe. It is proof that human creativity lives on despite bad theology and that, even after centuries of stony sleep, beauty can arise in places where humans have done their best to maintain its slumber.

Despite everything, humans are made in the image of God. We are creators, artists, problem-solvers, makers, and doers in our innermost beings. Of course, we're sinners, too. We drop bombs on each other, we exploit our neighbors, oppress the vulnerable, and destroy creation, but the stained glass windows in Zurich give me hope on my worst days and certainty on my best that in the end, the God in whose image humans are made always gets the last laugh.

Conclusion

Toward a Thoughtful Spirituality

The journey from Oakland, California, to the abbey on the Isle of Iona is long and it's complicated. When I traveled to Iona during the last days of writing this book, my dear wife drove me to a subway that I took to San Francisco International Airport. From there I flew to Manchester, England, and from Manchester I traveled by train to Oban, on the west coast of Scotland by way of Shrewsbury and East Kilbride, Scotland. At Oban I caught a ferry to Craignore on the Isle of Mull. From Craignore I took a two-hour bus ride across Mull to Fionnphort, where I caught another ferry that conveyed me across two kilometers of water to the Isle of Iona. Once on Iona, a guy named Peter met me and drove me to the Iona Abbey in an old green Volkswagen van. It was a difficult trip, and a little bit foolhardy, but I am hardly the first person to cross oceans at considerable expense to arrive on Iona because of a desire to make a deeper connection with the Divine, and, as a pilgrim in search of holiness, I was, like thousands before me, participating in a living expression of an ancient tradition.

I made my pilgrimage to Iona in November, a month when the wind howls in the islands off the west coast of Scotland.

More often than not, that wind is mixed with rain that lashes against the abbey's ancient walls; when the wind is strong enough (which frequently it is), it drives raindrops straight through the wooden frames of the abbey's east-facing windows. It was the weather that drew me to Iona. In California we were enduring the deepest drought in more than a thousand years, and as our reservoirs dwindled to the size of large mud puddles and as vast swaths of farmland lay fallow and parched, a high pressure system kept daytime winter temperatures comfortably up in the seventies. It was the most pleasant of natural disasters, but I longed for weather that would stir my soul and remind me of the less cruel, wild side of nature, and of nature's God. For weather that touches the soul, there may be no better place than the islands off Scotland's western coast, and for a place with a landscape that points to God, there may be nowhere more powerful than the Isle of Iona.

Iona is a sacred island, a place the Celtic Christians, like their pagan forebears, considered to be a "thin" place. This means that on Iona, the veil between heaven and earth is thin and permeable. The island itself is rugged and populated more by sheep than by humans. A small village greets the visitor at the place where the ferry from Mull makes landfall, but for the most part Iona is an island of granite outcroppings and moors covered in heather. Iona's beaches are white and sandy, except for one beach at the southern tip, which is covered in cobbles and seaweed that the sheep enjoy eating as they dodge breakers, their hoofs uneasy on stones polished smooth by the waves.

According to tradition, Iona is the place where, in 563 CE (or thereabouts), the Christian faith first made an appearance in Scotland when an Irish monk named St. Columba, together with a group of followers, left his homeland in a coracle (which is a round boat with no keel) not knowing for sure where he'd end up when he reached the far side of whatever oceans he might cross. Some traditions suggest St. Columba left Ireland after he got in trouble for stealing and copying a manuscript that belonged to someone else (an offense so serious, apparently, that it started a bloody battle).

That may or may not be the case, but for whatever reason, Columba left Ireland.

Apparently going off blindly into the ocean in an open, unnavigable boat was not an uncommon thing for Irish monks to do, and Columba was lucky not to have set off from Ireland's north coast, for the Atlantic is wide. In a matter of days—or perhaps weeks (as opposed to months or perhaps never, had he gone in another direction), Columba and his fellow travelers made landfall on the above-mentioned rocky beach where sheep eat seaweed while scrambling across cobbles to avoid the surf.

After landing on Iona, Columba climbed the highest hill on the island to see if Ireland was still visible off in the distance. Once assured that Ireland lay comfortably beneath the southern horizon, Columba and his fellow travelers set about establishing a monastic community on the island. The community grew, and in time it became one of medieval Europe's most prominent monastic communities, a place of scholarship and learning where monks copied and preserved important manuscripts and books and where the kings and nobles of Scotland, as well as some from Ireland and Norway, were laid to rest with their feet facing east to welcome the rising sun.

As political realities shifted, Irish monasticism fell from favor and, in 1203, the religious community on Iona affiliated itself with the Benedictine order. The Benedictines repaired and eventually rebuilt the ancient Irish abbey church in a gothic style, with pointed windows and a cruciform nave and transept.

In the sixteenth century, as Protestantism spread throughout Scotland, the monastic community on Iona disbanded, and the Benedictine abbey eventually fell into ruins, but the sense that Iona was a "thin" and sacred place remained in Europe's popular imagination. Felix Mendelssohn composed his *Hebrides Overture* while staying on Iona, and Samuel Johnson, upon visiting the island with his friend James Boswell, wrote,

> To abstract the mind from all local emotion would be impossible, if it were endeavored, and would be foolish if

it were possible. Whatever withdraws us from the power of our senses, whatever makes the past, the distant, or the future, predominate over the present, advances us in the dignity of thinking beings. Far from me, and from my friends, be such frigid philosophy as may conduct us indifferent and unmoved over any ground which has been dignified by wisdom, bravery or virtue. That man is little to be envied, whose patriotism would not gain force upon the plain of Marathon, or whose piety would not grow warmer among the ruins of Iona![1]

In Robert Louis Stevenson's novel *Kidnapped*, the protagonist, David Balfour, who has been abducted and shanghaied by an evil uncle intent upon stealing young David's inheritance, survives a shipwreck in the Iona sound and washes ashore on the tiny, uninhabited isle of Earraid, just to the south of Mull and about a mile across the water from Iona. Balfour nourishes himself by eating raw shellfish and finds the spiritual strength to survive by looking at the sacred island on the far side of the Iona sound:

> From a little up the hillside over the bay, I could catch a sight of the great, ancient church and the roofs of the people's houses in Iona . . . it kept hope alive, and helped me to eat my raw shell-fish (which had soon grown to be a disgust), and saved me from the sense of horror I had whenever I was quite alone with dead rocks, and fowls, and the rain, and the cold sea.[2]

After gazing upon the thinness of Iona, David Balfour turns to the east and begins the journey back to Edinburgh, there to collect his inheritance.

Visitors like Boswell and Johnson (in the eighteenth century), Mendelssohn and Stevenson (in the nineteenth century), and other prominent visitors (including Queen Victoria and Prince Albert) helped inspire a revival of interest in Iona, and in 1899 the Duke of Argyle set up a trust to oversee the rebuilding of the abbey church. In 1938, as the Great Depression devastated Scotland's economy, the Rev. George MacLeod, a

Church of Scotland minister serving one of Glasgow's most difficult parishes, started bringing unemployed shipbuilders to Iona to spend summers living in community and rebuilding the abbey's cloisters and residential areas. The work continued until 1967, by which time the abbey's cloisters, refectory, and residential wings all had been rebuilt. The work of reconstruction ended, but the community has continued to this day, with members of the Iona community in residence on the island and living in Glasgow, Edinburgh, and other cities throughout the UK, Europe, and the whole world. Those affiliated with the Iona community practice a discipline of prayer and of working to live a faith forged of deep spirituality and a passionate commitment to social justice.[3]

I cannot say, with any kind of objective certitude, that Iona actually is a thin place. The modern and rational side of me suspects that heaven and earth are equidistant at all points and that Iona isn't necessarily any holier than, say, Modesto, California. What I can say, however, is that Iona *feels* thin. I felt thinness in the several shades of green and gray that colored Iona's hills. I felt thinness as I walked among the ancient tombs of Scotland's long-forgotten nobility. I felt thinness in prayers and songs and meals shared with the Iona community. And I felt thinness when, late at night and during a storm, I went into the darkened abbey, sat down in the choir, and prayed while listening to the howl of gale-force winds that lashed and pounded against the ancient, sacred stones. In the book of 1 Kings, God speaks to the prophet Elijah not in the tempest, but in the still, small voice; on Iona, I heard God's voice speaking though the thinness of a storm.

I want to believe that Iona is a thin place, but I also want to believe that thin places like Iona can be found throughout the world. I want further to believe that any place can be made thinner through the practice of a thoughtful faith. When scientific observations and empirical data inform religious practice, the veil between heaven and earth grows thin because such information opens our eyes to what is real and to evidence of God's creative Spirit alive in creation. It allows the faithful to practice a richer, more life-giving stewardship of the world we are privileged to call home.

When Christians engage thoughtfully with the traditions of our faith, we narrow the gap between earth and heaven by rejecting those parts of our story that are violent, unkind, bigoted, coldhearted, outdated, outmoded, and stupid while embracing all of the life-affirming wisdom, beauty, grace, love, hope, and joy that have sustained the people of God for centuries. When with thoughtfulness we lift up our voices with prophetic conviction, speaking on behalf of the poor, the vulnerable, the mistreated, and the sore beset, we are chipping away the thickness through which so many of God's children experience the separation between heaven and earth.

When Christians are thoughtful in our interaction with new ideas, fresh insights, cultural shifts, and technological innovations, we remain open to the ways God's Spirit is alive in the world, thereby inviting the Divine to dwell in closer proximity to humanity. When we seek wisdom, our faith is informed by truths that must come from the far side of the veil. When we embrace mystery, we understand that as earth moves closer to heaven, the more we learn the less we will comprehend. Such awareness will inevitably make us humble, and our humility will guard against a thick separation between earthly landscapes and God's country.

When the practice of a thoughtful faith enables us to change and when, as changed people, our thoughtfulness inspires us to work for change that benefits others, then the veil is permeable indeed. And when, through the thinness, we glimpse a vision of heaven and are motivated thoughtfully to live lives that create beauty on earth, then the veil, already grown thin, starts to tear.

IN STORM AND IN SUNSHINE

I stayed five days on Iona, living and praying in the abbey with members of the Iona community and discussing Ignatian spirituality with five other pilgrims who, like me, had traveled to

Scotland's most sacred island to meet God in the thinness of the place. For four days the wind blew with gale force and the rain fell horizontally. When we left the shelter of the abbey, we needed to lean into the weather lest a gust of wind knock us down. Inside the abbey the noise of the storm was, at times, deafening, and sometimes the ancient stones in the abbey's walls seemed to groan under the strain of staying erect.

Then, as if by magic, in the afternoon of the last day of my Iona sojourn, the wind subsided, the clouds parted, and the island was bathed in the soft light and long shadows of November in northern latitudes. To the greens and grays that gave Iona a solemn beauty, the sunlight added gold. Suddenly, the cliffs of Mull and the mountain peaks of the Scottish Highlands became visible to the east. To the north and west I could see the contours of more than a dozen islands in the Inner Hebrides. All over the island, the sky was filled with birds who for days had been cowering safely on the ground, unwilling to take flight lest they be blown out to sea, and the God who seemed so alive in the fury of the storm danced in the beauty of a glorious autumn day in the Scottish isles.

God appears in an untold variety of ways, always making thin the veil between heaven and earth. The God who is equally alive in storm and in sunshine almost certainly does not need our help in the ongoing work of keeping heaven and earth in close company, but as a joyful expression of God's grace, we are invited to play a part in thinning the veil, a happy task made easier when we practice a thoughtful faith.

Notes

Introduction

1. For more information on the Pew Forum on Religion and Public Life, see http://www.pewforum.org/US-Religious-Knowledge-An-Overview-of-the-Pew-Forum-Survey-Results-and-Implications.aspx.

2. http://news.nationalgeographic.com/news/2006/05/0502_060502_geography.html.

3. The idea that the life of the mind is an essential component to faith is at least as old as the Gospels, which tell of Jesus instructing his followers to love God with their minds. Whereas the book of Deuteronomy tells of Moses instructing the people to love God with heart, soul, and strength, the Gospel according to Matthew has Jesus instructing his followers to love God with heart, soul, and mind; Mark and Luke remember Jesus saying "you shall love the Lord your God with all your heart," soul, mind, and strength. No one really knows why Jesus misquoted Moses, but one suspects he valued thoughtfulness and hoped his followers would do the same.

4. George M. Marsden, *Fundamentalism and American Culture: The Shaping of Twentieth-Century Evangelicalism: 1870–1925* (Oxford: Oxford University Press, 1982), 3–10.

5. Here it must be noted that evangelical Christianity is a broad movement. Not all evangelicals reject evolutionary biology and many evangelicals are dedicated to the work of curbing the effects of global warming. Not all evangelicals reject the HPV vaccination, and a growing minority of evangelicals understand that sexual orientation is not predicated on mental health. However, such attitudes—each in its own way a rejection of modern scientific knowledge—are prevalent among the ranks of American evangelicals.

6. Martin Luther King Jr., "Letter from a Birmingham Jail," http://www.africa.upenn.edu/Articles_Gen/Letter_Birmingham.html.

Chapter 1: The Accidental Schism

1. Charles Darwin, *The Correspondence of Charles Darwin* 8, 1860 (Cambridge: Cambridge University Press, 1993), 224, cited in Sara Joan Miles, "Charles Darwin and Asa Gray Discuss Teleology and Design," *American Scientific Affiliation*, September 2001, http://www.asa3.org/ASA/PSCF/2001/PSCF9-01Miles.html#10

2. William K. Seldon, *Princeton Theological Seminary: A Narrative History 1812–1992* (Princeton: Princeton University Press, 1992), 21–24.

3. John Calvin, *Commentaries on the First Book of Moses Called Genesis* (Grand Rapids: Baker Books, 2009), 86.

4. Origen of Alexandria, *De Principiis* Book IV.16, published online by New Advent, http://www.newadvent.org/fathers/04124.htm.

5. J. David Pleins, *The Evolving God: Charles Darwin on the Naturalness of Religion* (New York: Bloomsbury Academic, 2013), Kindle version, location 779.

6. David B. Williams, "A Wrangle Over Darwin: How Evolution Evolved in America," *Harvard Magazine,* September 1998, http://www.harvardmagazine.com/1998/09/darwin.html.

7. Population and median household income numbers for Dayton, TN, can be found at http://www.city-data.com/city/Dayton-Tennessee.html; information on the federally designated poverty level can be found on the United States' Department of Health and Human Services website: http://www.dhs.ri.gov/Portals/0/Uploads/Documents/Public/General%20DHS/FPL.pdf.

8. Bruce Bawer, *Stealing Jesus: How Fundamentalism Betrays Jesus* (New York: Crown Publishers, 1997), 124.

9. George M. Marsden, *Fundamentalism and American Culture: The Shaping of Twentieth-Century Evangelicalism: 1870–1925* (New York: Oxford University Presss, 1982), 185.

10. Ibid.

11. Garin Hovannisian, "A Book for No Seasons: The Forgotten Aspects of John Scopes's Famous Biology Textbook," *The Weekly Standard,* July 12, 2007, http://www.weeklystandard.com/Content/Public/Articles/000/000/013/862heeyk.asp.

12. George William Hunter, *A Civic Biology Presented in Problems* (New York: American Book Company, 1914), 261–63.

13. Lita Cosner, "How Does the Bible Teach 6,000 Years?" Creation.com, http://creation.com/6000-years.

Chapter 2: Respecting Empirical Data

1. For a full text of Leonardo DiCaprio's address to the United Nations see Leonardo DiCaprio, "Leonardo DiCaprio at the UN: 'Climate Change Is Not Hysteria—It's a Fact,'" *The Guardian,* Sept. 23, 2014, http://www.theguardian.com/environment/2014/sep/23 /leonarodo-dicaprio-un-climate-change-speech-new-york.

2. Arieh O'Sullivan, "World's First Skyscraper Sought to Intimidate Masses," *Jerusalem Post,* Feb. 14, 2011, http://www.jpost.com/Video -Articles/Video/Worlds-first-skyscraper-sought-to-intimidate-masses.

3. See Josh. 6.

4. Jonathan Sarfati, "How Old is the Earth?" Creation.com, http:// creation.com/how-old-is-the-earth.

5. Mark A. Stein, "'Redwood Summer': It Was Guerrilla Warfare: Conservation: Protesters' Anti-logging Tactics Fail to Halt North Coast Timber Harvest. Encounters Leave Loggers Resentful," *Los Angeles Times,* Sept. 2, 1990, http://articles.latimes.com/1990-09-02/news /mn-2050_1_north-coast.

6. That other lumber companies joined Pacific Lumber Company in the practice of clear-cutting is something I write not as a researcher or a historian but as an eyewitness. At the time I could see clear-cutting in the Albion River watershed from my bedroom window; clear-cutting was an issue people in my hometown talked about all the time. It seems that Maxxam proved a lumber company could clear-cut, pay all the government-imposed fines incurred for the illegal process, and still make a huge profit. This was the manifestation of Reaganomics behind the Redwood Curtain.

7. Cheryl Sullivan, "California Redwoods Embattled Anew. Clear-Cutting Controversy," *The Christian Science Monitor,* Nov. 18, 1987, http://www.csmonitor.com/1987/1118/acut.html.

8. The Forest Foundation, "Restoring Redwood Forests," http:// www.calforestfoundation.org/pdf/RESTORING-REDWOOD -FORESTS.pdf.

9. NASA, "Consensus: 97% of Climate Scientists Agree," Global Climate Change: Vital Signs of the Planet, http://climate.nasa.gov /scientific-consensus/.

10. Tiffany Germain with Ryan Koronowski, "The Anti-Science Climate Denier Caucus: 113th Congress Edition," *Climate Progress,* June 26, 2013, http://thinkprogress.org/climate/2013/06/26/2202141 /anti-science-climate-denier-caucus-113th-congress-edition/.

11. "Climate-related disasters have cost half a trillion dollars since world leaders last met to discuss climate change," *Oxfam America,* September 18, 2014, http://www.oxfamamerica.org/press/climate -related-disasters-have-cost-half-a-trillion-dollars-since-world-leaders -last-met-to-discuss-climate-change/.

12. Richard A. Lovett, "Antarctica's 'Ghost' Mountains Explained," *National Geographic News,* November 16, 2011, http://news .nationalgeographic.com/news/2011/11/111116-antarctica-mountains -mystery-ice-science-earth/.

13. "The Battle for the Coast," *World Ocean Review,* http:// worldoceanreview.com/en/wor-1/coasts/living-in-coastal-areas/.

14. Lilian Yamamoto and Miguel Esteban, "Atoll Islands and Climate Change: Disappearing States?" *United Nations University,* March 1, 2012, http://unu.edu/publications/articles/atoll-islands-and -climate-change-disappearing-states.html#info.

15. "Warming Climate to Hit Bangladesh Hard with Sea Level Rise, More Floods and Cyclones, World Bank Report Says," The World Bank, June 19, 2013, http://www.worldbank.org/en/news/press -release/2013/06/19/warming-climate-to-hit-bangladesh-hard-with -sea-level-rise-more-floods-and-cyclones-world-bank-report-says.

16. Stewart Brand, *Whole Earth Discipline* (New York: Viking, 2009), 10.

17. For more on this, see T. H. Gaster, "Cosmogony," *Interpreters' Dictionary of the Bible,* vol. 1, 702–9 (Nashville: Abingdon Press, 1989).

18. This happened on September 13, 2014, damn it, but the Giants are still the awesomer of the two teams: they went on to win the World Series.

Chapter 3: Wrestling with Tradition

1. Jeff Maslen, "More Countries Are Asking Whether They Produce Too Many PhDs, Says New Report," *The Chronicle of Higher Education,* April 10, 2013, http://chronicle.com/article/Report-Examines-the-Global/138439/.

2. Williston Walker et al., *A History of the Christian Church,* 4th ed. (New York: Charles Scribner's Sons, 1985), 283.

3. María Rosa Menocal, *The Ornament of the World* (New York: Back Bay Books, 2002), 97.

4. Joseph F. O'Callaghan, *Reconquest and Crusade in Medieval Spain* (Philadelphia: University of Pennsylvania Press, 2003), 193.

5. The information about St. James and his shrine at Santiago de Comopstela is widely available both in print and online. However,

while writing about the history of Santiago here I found myself returning again and again to Chris Lowney, *A Vanished World: Muslims, Christians and Jews in Medieval Spain* (New York: Oxford University Press, 2006). The book is as informative as it is well-written.

6. I'm referring here to Ps. 137. Many of us sing the opening verse, perhaps to a lively reggae beat:

By the rivers of Babylon—
there we sat down and there we wept
when we remembered Zion.

I doubt anyone, however, has ever sung the final verses:

O daughter Babylon, you devastator!
Happy shall they be who pay you back
what you have done to us!
Happy shall they be who take your little ones
and dash them against the rock!

7. Hubert Herring, *A History of Latin America from the Beginnings to the Present*, 3rd ed. (New York: Alfred A. Knopf, 1969), 170.

8. See, for example, Rodney Stark, *God's Battalions* (San Francisco: HarperOne, 2010).

9. Zoé Oldenbourg, *The Crusades* (New York: Pantheon Books, 1966), 44.

10. Ibid., i.

11. I wrote these words while riding in the passenger seat of our family minivan. From time to time people ask me how I have time to be both a writer and a pastor. Several factors go into my being able to do both jobs with reasonable success: (1) I don't own a television, (2) I don't play golf, (3) I am married to someone who likes to drive more than I do and who doesn't mind it when I sit in the passenger seat with my nose buried in my laptop, and (4) I seldom get carsick.

12. The full text of all these hymns, which are in the public domain, can be found at hymnary.org.

13. See, for example, George H. W. Bush's speech to a joint session of Congress at the end of the Gulf War, which can be found on the website of the University of Virginia's Miller Center, http://millercenter.org/president/speeches/detail/3430.

14. For more on the National Prayer Breakfast and the Fellowship Foundation that organizes it, see Jeff Sharlet, *The Family* (New York: Harper Collins, 2009).

15. U.S. Government Printing Office, "Public Papers of the Presidents of the United States: George H. W. Bush (1991, Book I)," January 31, 1991, 85–86, http://www.gpo.gov/fdsys/pkg/PPP-1991 -book1/html/PPP-1991-book1-doc-pg85-2.htm.

16. See, for example, "A Call to the Churches" in *Episcopal Press and News*, found on the website of the Archives of the Episcopal Church, http://www.episcopalarchives.org/cgi-bin/ENS/ENSpress_release .pl?pr_number=91043.

17. Peter Steinfels, "War in the Gulf: The Home Front; Church Leaders Reaffirm Opposition to War," *New York Times*, Feb. 15, 1991, http://www.nytimes.com/1991/02/15/us/war-in-the-gulf-the-home -front-church-leaders-reaffirm-opposition-to-war.html.

18. Graham's stay at the White House on the night the war began is documented in many places, including in the National Prayer Breakfast speech referenced above.

19. Jim Lobe, "Conservative Christians Biggest Backers of Iraq War," Inter Press Service News Agency, Oct. 10, 2002, http://www.ipsnews .net/2002/10/politics-us-conservative-christians-biggest-backers-of-iraq-war/.

20. Meredith Bennett-Smith, "Pat Robertson, Islamophobic Televangelist, Compares 'Evil' Islam To Nazism (VIDEO)," *Huffington Post*, April 23, 2013, http://www.huffingtonpost.com/2013/04/23/pat -robertson-islam-nazism-evil-video_n_3134711.html.

21. Walid Shoebat, "The Armies of the Antichrist Are Near, and Russia Will Take the Victory," Feb. 23, 2014, http://shoebat.com/2014/02/23 /armies-antichrist-near-russia-will-take-victory-part-1/.

22. Drew Griffin and Kathleen Johnston, "'Ex-terrorist' Rakes in Homeland Security Bucks," CNN, July 14, 2011, http://www.cnn .com/2011/US/07/11/terrorism.expert/.

23. Chris Hedges, "The War against Tolerance," *Truthdig*, Feb. 11, 2008, http://www.truthdig.com/report/item/20080211_the_war _against_tolerance#.

24. For an excellent article detailing the efforts of evangelicals to transform the United States military into a force of spiritual warriors, see Jeff Sharlet, "Jesus Killed Mohammad," *Harpers Magazine*, May 2009. A longer version of the article can be found under the title "The War" in Jeff Sharlet, *C Street: The Fundamentalist Threat to American Democracy*, 204–57 (New York: Little, Brown and Company, 2010).

25. Tertullian, *Of the Crown*, http://www.tertullian.org/lfc/LFC10 -11_de_corona.htm.

26. Origen of Alexandria, *Contra Celsus,* chap. 73, http://www
.newadvent.org/fathers/04168.htm.

27. Augustine of Hippo, *The City of God,* chap. 7, http://www
.newadvent.org/fathers/120119.htm.

28. Thomas Aquinas, *Summa Theologica,* part 2, question 40, http://
www.newadvent.org/summa/3040.htm..

29. John Calvin, "Fourth Sermon on Deuteronomy 20:16–20,"
in *The Legacy of John Calvin: Some Actions for the Church in the 21st
Century,* ed. Setri Nyomi (Geneva: The World Alliance of Reformed
Churches and the John Knox International Reformed Center,
2008), 59.

30. Historians may quibble: the First World War didn't happen
in a vacuum, but was set up by various wars that preceded it. It was,
however, the first major conflict on the twentieth century's world stage.

Chapter 4: Learning from What Is Old

1. Samuel Kobia, "Bible Is the 'Ultimate Immigration
Handbook,'" *World Council of Churches,* June 15, 2009, http://
www.oikoumene.org/en/press-centre/news/bible-is-the-ultimate
-immigration-handbook.

2. For a discussion of the biblical mandate to care for immigrants,
see my book *Neighbor: Christian Encounters with "Illegal" Immigration*
(Louisville, KY: Westminster John Knox Press, 2010), 13–24.

3. At their request, I'm not using Job's or Dolores's real names;
for reasons that should become apparent by the time I'm done telling
their story, I chose to give him the name of the long-suffering biblical
character and her a name that means "suffering" and that is usually
associated with Mary, the mother of Jesus.

4. Rafael Romo and Nick Thompson, "Inside San Pedro Sula, the
'Murder Capital' of the World," CNN, March 28, 2013, http://www
.cnn.com/2013/03/27/world/americas/honduras-murder-capital/.

5. Tracy Wilkinson, "In Honduras, Rival Gangs Keep a Death
Grip on San Pedro Sula," *Los Angeles Times,* Dec. 17, 2013, http://
www.latimes.com/world/la-fg-c1-honduras-violence-20131216-dto
-htmlstory.html.

6. Such as Lev. 19:33–34.

7. I visited such a camp in March of 1986 while on a high school
Spanish club trip to Costa Rica.

8. United Nations High Commissioner for Refugees, *Convention and Protocol Relating to the Status of Refugees,* http://www.unhcr.org/3b66c2aa10.html.

9. "Barrio 18 (M-18)," *Insight Crime: Organized Crime in the Americas,* http://www.insightcrime.org/honduras-organized-crime-news/barrio-18-honduras.

10. The United Nations High Commissioner for Refugees, *Children on the Run: Unaccompanied Children Leaving Central America and Mexico and the Need for International Protection,* March 12, 2014, http://www.unhcrwashington.org/sites/default/files/1_UAC_Children%20On%20the%20Run_Executive%20Summary.pdf.

11. Ibid.

12. Jill Replogle, "Escondido Planning Commission Rejects Shelter for Immigrant Children," KPBS.org, June 25, 2014, http://www.kpbs.org/news/2014/jun/25/escondido-planning-commission-votes-down-shelter-i/.

13. Matt Hansen and Mark Boster, "Protesters in Murrieta Block Detainees' Buses in Tense Standoff," *Los Angeles Times,* July 1, 2014, http://www.latimes.com/local/lanow/la-me-ln-immigrants-murrieta-20140701-story.html#page=1.

14. Karen Kapsidelis, "Plan to Use Saint Paul's to Shelter Immigrant Children Dropped," *Richmond Times Dispatch,* June 20, 2014, http://www.timesdispatch.com/news/state-regional/plan-to-use-saint-paul-s-to-shelter-immigrant-children/article_ce549712-f4d3-5721-86ca-4ad76aa1ad8c.html.

15. Christopher Sherman and Jennifer Agiesta, "Poll: Immigration Concerns Rise with Tide of Kids," *AP: The Big Story,* July 29, 2014, http://bigstory.ap.org/article/poll-immigration-concerns-rise-tide-kids.

Chapter 5: Learning from What Is New

1. Brooke Foss Westcott, *The Epistles of St. John* (Cambridge and London: Macmillan and Co., 1892), 318.

2. Acts 10.

3. Acts 8:32b–33, quoting Isa. 53:7–8.

4. Isa. 56:3–5. Incidentally the promise to give eunuchs an "everlasting name *that shall not be cut off*" is evidence that the prophet had a fairly twisted sense of humor.

5. See Acts 15.

6. Gal. 5:12. Paul's sense of humor was not unlike that of the prophet Isaiah.

7. To be fair, I know Christians from India who still wonder—and argue about—whether or not it is OK to eat food that's been offered up to Hindu deities, but that is a necessary discussion in their context. Most non-Indian Christians have never really had to face this issue.

8. There are several examples of a woman being her father's property until married; a particularly powerful one is found is Deut. 22:19, when a man who slanders his bride must pay one hundred shekels to the woman's father. But from stories of women married to the patriarchs to the New Testament's unequivocal assertion that the husband is the head of the wife, the idea that women are the property of their fathers and husbands is universal and seldom—if ever—challenged in the Bible.

9. Exod. 22:16–17.

10. Exod. 21:7–11.

11. Deut. 22:28–29.

Chapter 6: Embracing the Unknown

1. Wendell Berry, "The Burden of the Gospels," in *The Way of Ignorance and Other Essays* (Berkeley, CA: Shoemaker & Hoard, 2005), 132.

2. Lewis was also a prolific and well-respected scholar of sixteenth- and seventeenth-century English literature, but I don't know if many Christians who aren't students of Edmund Spenser and John Donne ever read his scholarly work.

3. "Energy" is a word we would have used in my countercultural childhood behind the Redwood Curtain, on California's north coast. "Personality" is probably a more accurate word for what this particular band of heretics believed about Jesus. But in my own particular brand of heresy, Jesus, like John the Baptist before him, was a hippie, so I'm sticking with "energy."

4. There was one Anabaptist splinter group that engaged in armed rebellion against those who were persecuting them. The rebellion was put down, and all of its leaders were burned at the stake. Since then, pretty much every movement within the Anabaptist tradition has stuck to pacifism.

5. Matt. 5:10–12.

6. "Charlie Hebdo: Gun Attack on French Magazine Kills 12," *BBC*, Jan. 7, 2015 http://www.bbc.com/news/world-europe-30710883.

7. For a summary of the *Charlie Hebdo* attacks, see "Charlie Hebdo Attack: Three Days of Terror," BBC News, Jan. 14, 2015, http://www .bbc.com/news/world-europe-30708237.

8. Naina Bajekal, "Mosques Attacked in France Following *Charlie Hebdo* Attack," *Time*, Jan. 8, 2015, http://time.com/3659177/attacks -mosques-charlie-hebdo/.

9. Asma Ajroudi, "Charlie Hebdo Attack: A Turning Point for Islamophobia in France?" Al Arabiya News, Jan. 10, 2015, http://english .alarabiya.net/en/perspective/analysis/2015/01/10/Charlie-Hebdo-attack -A-turning-point-for-Islamophobia-in-France-.html.

Chapter 7: Loving Knowledge

1. Augustine of Hippo, *The Confessions of Saint Augustine*, trans. Hal M. Helms (Orleans, MA: Paraclete Press, 1986), 238.

2. "Aren't There Enough Islamofascists in America Trying to Sell Their Crap Sandwich that Islam Is a Religion of Peace?" *Bare Naked Islam*, Sept. 6, 2013, http://www.barenakedislam.com/2013/09/06 /arent-there-enough-islamofascists-in-america-trying-to-sell-their-crap -sandwich-that-islam-is-a-religion-of-peace/.

3. Ishaan Tharoor, "U.A.E.'s First Female Fighter Pilot Dropped Bombs on the Islamic State," *The Washington Post*, Sept. 25, 2014, http://www.washingtonpost.com/blogs/worldviews/wp/2014/09 /25/u-a-e-s-first-female-fighter-pilot-dropped-bombs-on-the-islamic -state/.

4. For these and other fun, reality-based facts about Islam, see my book *The Search for Truth about Islam* (Louisville, KY: Westminster John Knox Press, 2013).

5. Material from the two preceding paragraphs was excerpted from a study guide I wrote for *The Jesus Fatwa*, a video curriculum produced by Living the Questions. It appears here with the permission of Living the Questions. For more information on *The Jesus Fatwa*, please visit jesusfatwah.com.

6. Nathan Lean, *The Islamophobia Industry: How the Right Manufactures Fear of Muslims* (London: Pluto Press, 2012), 39.

7. Ibid., xi–xii.

8. My presentation of humanism is distilled from Williston Walker et al., *A History of the Christian Church*, 4th ed. (New York: Charles Scribner's Sons, 1985), 392–94, 405–15.

9. T. H. L. Parker, *John Calvin: A Biography* (Philadelphia: Westminster Press, 1975), xiii–xv.

10. Ibid., 30–31.

11. Prov. 8:22–31.

12. John 1:1–5.

Chapter 8: The Thoughtfully Changing Community

1. Mark Twain, "The Innocents Abroad," Project Gutenberg, http://www.gutenberg.org/files/3176/3176-h/3176-h.htm.

2. Astute readers will note my approval of the church's decision—expressed in the story of Jesus's conversation with the Lebanese woman—to expand beyond the confines of Judaism by accepting Gentile believers as full members of the household of faith. This enthusiasm for inclusion should not be misunderstood as a criticism of Judaism or of Jews—those living in the first century or those alive and practicing their faith today. The extent to which any of Jesus' fellow Jews may or may not have shared his xenophobia or would have approved of his lack of tact in calling a Lebanese child a dog is unknown to me, and it is beyond the purview of this book. Besides, given Christendom's track record on such matters, no Christian has much moral high ground to disparage a person of another faith for failing to show kindness to outsiders and nonbelievers, especially if that person happens to be Jewish.

3. S. L. Greenslade, trans. and ed., *Early Latin Theology*, Library of Christian Classics 5 (Philadelphia: Westminster Press, 1956), 226–28.

4. Ibid., 232.

5. It's worth noting that sometimes Ambrose used the power of the Church for just and righteous ends. Two years after the incident at Calinicum, the Roman emperor Theodosius ordered the slaughter of 7,000 unarmed denizens of Thessalonica, a city in Greece with a reputation for unrest. In response, Ambrose excommunicated the emperor, who then submitted himself to the humiliation of public penance for his crime. The punishment was not, perhaps, sufficient, but it was as strong a censure as anyone ever could hope to inflict upon an emperor of Rome, and it remains one of the historical Church's great moments of public witness. The drama of history is complicated, and so are the characters who play on its stage. For more information on the slaughter at Thessalonica and to read Ambrose's letter of reprimand to Theodosius, see *Early Latin Theology*, 251–58.

6. Williston Walker et al., *A History of the Christian Church,* 4th ed. (New York: Charles Scribner's Sons, 1985), 286.

7. Zoé Oldenbourg, *The Crusades* (New York: Pantheon Books, 1966), 465.

8. "The 1190 Massacre," *History of York,* http://www.historyofyork .org.uk/themes/norman/the-1190-massacre.

9. Jonathan Kirsch, *The Grand Inquisitor's Manual* (San Francisco: HarperOne, 2008), 167–205.

10. While I didn't read Luther's book, I found this excerpt online at "Anti-Semitism: Martin Luther's 'The Jews & Their Lies' (1543)," *The Jewish Virtual Library,* https://www.jewishvirtuallibrary.org/jsource /anti-semitism/Luther_on_Jews.html.

11. The First Assembly of the World Council of Churches, "The Christian Approach to the Jews," *Jewish-Christian Relations,* http://www.jcrelations.net/The+Christian+Approach+to+the+Jews .2584.0.html?L=3.

12. The Third Assembly of the World Council of Churches, "A Resolution on Antisemitism," *Jewish-Christian Relations,* http:// www.jcrelations.net/A_Resolution_on_Antisemitism.1510.0.html?L =3&page=1.

13. Declaration on the relation of the Church to Non-Christian Religions *Nostra Aetate* Proclaimed by His Holiness Pope Paul VI, on October 28, 1965. http://www.vatican.va/archive/hist_councils /ii_vatican_council/documents/vat-ii_decl_19651028_nostra-aetate _en.html.

14. Christian and Jewish supporters of Israel's policies of occupation in Palestinian territories often accuse people like me of anti-Semitism because we criticize policies that seem—to us, anyway—to be racist, unjustifiably violent, and against the cause of peace. While some of Israel's critics certainly are anti-Semitic, most aren't. In order to accurately characterize every criticism of Israel's policies as "anti-Semitism," it would need to be established, first, that there is an inherent and organic connection between Judaism and the state of Israel and, second, that Jews—and therefore Israel—are incapable of developing and implementing policies that merit opposition.

Chapter 9: Political Engagement

1. H. Richard Niebuhr, *Christ and Culture* (New York: Harper & Brothers, 1954), 8–9.

2. For the record, I did end up writing about my stay in the South of France in my Islam book. See chapter 7 of *The Search for Truth About Islam: A Christian Pastor Separates Fact From Fiction* (Louisville, KY: Westminster John Knox Press, 2013).

3. Again for the record (and in my defense), a year later my wife and I spent a lovely week together in Annecy, Haute-Savoie, celebrating our twentieth anniversary.

4. Dennis Prager, "Presbyterian Church Defames Christianity," *The Dennis Prager Show*, July 20, 2004, http://www.dennisprager.com /presbyterian-church-defames-christianity/.

5. Alan Dershowitz, "Presbyterians Shameful Boycott," *Los Angeles Times*, Aug. 4, 2004, http://articles.latimes.com/2004/aug/04/opinion /oe-dershowitz4.

6. There are plenty of secular folks on the far left, and there are some progressive Christians who try to create a counterbalance to the religious right, but believe me: as liberal as I am, I would know if there were a progressive analogue to the American religious right.

7. C. C. J. Carpenter et al., "Public Statement by Eight Alabama Clergymen," MassResistance, http://www.massresistance.org/docs /gen/09a/mlk_day/statement.html.

8. Martin Luther King Jr., "Letter from a Birmingham Jail," African Studies Center, University of Pennsylvania, http://www.africa .upenn.edu/Articles_Gen/Letter_Birmingham.html.

9. Ibid.

10. Both the quote and the inspiration for the preceding paragraph are taken from chapter 16 of Robert McAfee Brown, *The Spirit of Protestantism* (New York: Oxford University Press, 1961). The quote is found on page 202. I've changed the quote slightly, making it gender-inclusive. I met Bob Brown thirty years after he wrote these words, and while we were never intimate friends, we maintained a friendly, collegial relationship for the final decade of his life. I am confident he would appreciate the edit.

11. Some astute readers will point out that, technically, Israel has not occupied the Gaza Strip since 2005, when it withdrew all of its troops from and dismantled its settlements in the coastal Palestinian enclave. However, what Israel does not occupy from within it controls from without.

12. "The Companies," *WeDivest.org*, https://wedivest.org/companies.

13. Jeff Karub and Rachael Zoll, "Presbyterians to Divest as Protest against Israel," *The Big Story*, June 21, 2014, http://bigstory.ap.org /article/presbyterians-divest-protest-against-israel.

14. Anti-Defamation League, "Press Release: ADL Disappointed by Presbyterian Church's Decision to Support Divestment from Israel" July 20, 2014, http://www.adl.org/press-center/press-releases/interfaith/ado-disappointed-presbyterian-church-decision-israel-divestment.html.

15. "Netanyahu Blasts Presbyterian Divestment as 'Disgraceful,'" *Haaretz,* June 22, 2014, http://www.haaretz.com/news/diplomacy-defense/.premium-1.600437.

16. Jodi Rudoren and Isabel Kershner, "Israel's Search for 3 Missing Teens Ends in Grief," *The New York Times,* June 30, 2014, http://www.nytimes.com/2014/07/01/world/middleeast/Israel-missing-teenagers.html?_r=0.

17. Kareem Khadder, Greg Botelho, and Josh Levs, "Palestinian Teen's Abduction, Killing Intensifies Tensions in Mideast," CNN, July 3, 2014, http://www.cnn.com/2014/07/02/world/meast/mideast-tensions/.

18. The United Nations Office for the Coordination of Humanitarian Affairs, "Occupied Palestinian Territory: Gaza Emergency Situation Report (as of 5 August 2014, 0800 hrs)," Aug. 5, 2014, http://www.ochaopt.org/documents/ocha_opt_sitrep_05_08_2014.pdf.

19. Valerie Amos, "Briefing of the Under-Secretary-General Valerie Amos to the Security Council on the Situation in the Gaza Strip," United Nations Office for the Coordination of Humanitarian Affairs, July 31, 2014, https://docs.unocha.org/sites/dms/Documents/USG%20Amos%20SecCo%20statement%20on%20Gaza%20-%20 31%20July%202014%20-%20As%20delivered.pdf.

Chapter 10: Creative Embodiment

1. Bishop Ken Untener of Saginaw, "Archbishop Oscar Romero Prayer: A Step Along The Way," United States Conference of Catholic Bishops, http://www.usccb.org/prayer-and-worship/prayers-and-devotions/prayers/archbishop_romero_prayer.cfm.

2. Williston Walker et al., *A History of the Christian Church,* 4th ed. (New York: Charles Scribner's Sons, 1985), 444.

3. Question: If a megachurch gets big enough, does it become a gigachurch?

4. Dorothy L. Sayers, *The Mind of the Maker* (San Francisco: Harper San Francisco, 1987).

5. This dates me, but if you came of age among evangelicals in the 1980s, you know what I'm talking about here.

6. Dorothy L. Sayers, "Why Work," Center for Faith and Work at LeTorneau University, http://centerforfaithandwork.com/sites/default /files/Sayers%20Why%20Work.pdf.

7. That the Reagan administration supported the Contras using the proceeds of arms sales to Iran is common knowledge; the use of proceeds from the sale of crack cocaine in California is subject to debate. I've described it in the chapter above as settled fact for two reasons. First, I am convinced by the evidence collected by George Washington University's National Security Archive (http://www2.gwu.edu/~nsarchiv/NSAEBB/ NSAEBB2/nsaebb2.htm). Second, I encountered evidence of CIA drug trafficking firsthand on a visit to Guatemala in 1989.

8. http://www.seedsoflearning.org/.

9. I realize that my brother Morgan sort of drops out of the story once he gets married. Today he makes a living as a paramedic, and he has continued working as a singer/songwriter, often performing with our youngest sister, Gwyneth Moreland (http://www.gwynethmoreland .com/) in a locally successful band called Foxglove (https://www .facebook.com/foxgloveonline). Morgan also is a luthier, whose hand -made guitars are as beautiful to look at as they are to play (https://www .facebook.com/morgandanielguitars).

10. The United Nations High Commissioner for Refugees, *Children on the Run: Unaccompanied Children Leaving Central America and Mexico and the Need for International Protection*, Mar. 12, 2014, http:// www.unhcrwashington.org/sites/default/files/1_UAC_Children%20 On%20the%20Run_Executive%20Summary.pdf.

11. "Editorial: Privatization, Not Threats, Best Drought Action," *Orange County Register*, July 16, 2014, http://www.ocregister.com /articles/water-629065-state-government.html.

12. Greg Botelho, Jacque Wilson, and Ben Brumfield, "In Ebola Fight, Security Forces to Make Villagers Comply with Medical Plan," CNN, July 31, 2014, http://www.cnn.com/2014/07/30/health/ebola -american-aid-workers/.

13. Sarah Gray, "Stephen Colbert Needs a Drink: 'Things Might Actually Be as Bad as We Make Them Sound on Cable News,'" *Salon.com*, July 30, 2014, http://www.salon.com/2014/07/30/stephen _colbert_needs_a_drink_things_might_actually_be_as_bad_as_we _make_them_sound_on_cable_news/.

14. Ulrich Gerster, *The Windows of the Grossmünster Zürich* (Bern: Society for the History of Swiss Art, 2012), 2.

15. Ibid., 5–12.

Conclusion

1. James Boswell, *The Journal of a Tour to the Hebrides*, Undiscovered Scotland, http://www.undiscoveredscotland.co.uk/usebooks/boswell -hebrides/11-iona-mull.html.

2. Robert Louis Stevenson, *Kidnapped* (New York: Grosset & Dunlap, 1948), 138–39.

3. Much of my information on the history of Iona comes from anecdotes and from reading signs posted around the abbey by Historic Scotland. This information was confirmed and supplemented by my reading of Rosemary Power's *The Story of Iona* (Norwich: Canterbury Press, 2013).

CPSIA information can be obtained at www.IC~~~~~~~~~
Printed in the USA
LVOW10s0722290915

456063LV00003B/3/P

9 "780664 260644